BBC

T0351677

| TALK |

Japanese

YUKIKO ISONO &
LYNNE STRUGNELL
Series Editor: Alwena Lamping

Published by BBC Active, an imprint of Educational Publishers LLP, part of the Pearson Education Group, 80 Strand, London WC2R 0RL, England.

© Pearson Education LLP 2015

BBC logo © BBC 1996. BBC and BBC ACTIVE are trademarks of the British Broadcasting Corporation.

First published 1998.
Third edition 2015.
10

ISBN 978-1-406-68011-9

Publisher: Debbie Marshall
Edited by: Helen Wilson
Additional editing by: Sawako Irie
Additional material: Yuko Hashimoto
Project editor: Emma Brown
Illustrations: © Mark Duffin
Layout: DTP Media Ltd. www.dtp-media.co.uk
Cover design: Two Associates
Insides design: Nicolle Thomas and Rob Lian
Cover photograph: © iStock.com/juicybits
Audio producer: John Green, tefl tapes
Sound engineer: Tim Woolf
Presenters: Ryo Inoue, Sachiko Kuroiwa, Nana Takahashi, Peter Wickham
Studio: Robert Nichols Audio Productions
Music: Peter Hutchings

Printed and bound in Great Britain by Bell and Bain Ltd, Glasgow

The Publisher's policy is to use paper manufactured from sustainable forests.

Contents

Introduction

Welcome to the new edition of **Talk Japanese**, the bestselling course from BBC Active, which has inspired and helped so many people to learn Japanese from scratch and given them the confidence to have a go.

The key to **Talk Japanese**'s effectiveness is the successful **Talk** method, developed by experienced teachers of languages to adult beginners. Its structured and systematic approach encourages you to make genuine progress and promotes a real sense of achievement.

The choice of situations and vocabulary is based on the everyday needs of people travelling to Japan. The language is presented using *romaji*, the official Japanese system of using Roman script, i.e. the same alphabet as English, to represent the sounds of Japanese.

Talk Japanese includes a book and 120 minutes of recordings of Japanese native speakers. The book in this new edition has several additional features, inspired by feedback from users and teachers. There's an extended grammar section (pages 121–135), a two-way glossary (pages 136–144) and the ever-popular **Talk** *Wordpower* (pages 133–134), designed to increase your vocabulary fast.

Free tutors' support and activities are available online at www.bbcactivelanguages.com and there are additional resources on the BBC Languages website at www.bbc.co.uk/languages/japanese/.

How to make the most of Talk Japanese

Each of the ten units is completed in ten easy-to-follow steps.

1   Read the first page of the unit to focus on what you're aiming to learn and set it in context while gaining some relevant vocabulary.

2   Listen to the key phrases – don't be tempted to read them first. Then listen to them again, this time reading them in your book too. Finally, try reading them out loud before listening one more time.

Wherever you see this: **1•5**, the phrases or dialogues are recorded on the CD (i.e. CD1, track 5).

---

3 Work your way through the activities which follow the key phrases. These highlight key language elements and are carefully designed to develop your listening skills and your understanding of Japanese. You can check your answers at any time in the *Transcripts and answers*.

4 Read the *Nihongo de wa* explanations of how Japanese works as you come to them – this information is placed just where you need it. And if you'd like to know more, visit the relevant pages in the *Grammar* section, indicated by the following symbol: **G13** .

5 After completing the activities, and before you try the *Put it all together* section, listen to the conversations straight through. The more times you listen, the more familiar Japanese will become and the more comfortable you'll become with it. You might also like to read the dialogues at this stage – preferably out loud.

6 Complete the consolidation activities on the *Put it all together* page and check your answers with the *Transcripts and answers*.

7 Use the language you've learnt – the presenters on the audio will prompt you and guide you through the *Now you're talking!* page as you practise speaking Japanese.

8 Check your progress. First, test your knowledge with the *Quiz*. Then assess whether you can do everything on the checklist – if in doubt, go back and spend some more time on the relevant section.

9 Read the learning hint at the end of the unit, which provides ideas and suggestions on how to use your study time effectively or how to extend your knowledge.

10 Finally, relax and listen to the whole unit, understanding what the people are saying in Japanese and taking part in the conversations.

Pronunciation guide

Japanese is not difficult to pronounce. The best way to acquire a good accent is to listen to the audio often and to imitate the speakers closely.

1   Japanese vowels are consistent and pure sounds.

a	s**a**murai	as in	*J**a**pan*, **a**pple*
i	k**i**mono		*s**i**t*, **i**nk*
u	s**u**shi		*p**u**sh*, *b**u**sh*
e	karat**e**		*b**e**t*, *r**e**d*
o	Y**o**kohama		*b**o**ttom*, *b**o**ttle*

Long vowels, written **ā**, **ii**, **ū**, **ē**, **ō**, have the same sound which is held for twice as long.

2   Most **consonants** are similar in Japanese and English but the following need attention:

f + u or **e**	Much softer than an English *f*, rather like pursing the lips and gently breathing out.
r	This sound is written *r* when using Roman letters, but is actually between *l* and *r*.
ch	Always pronounced softly, as in **ch**urch*.

Double consonants are pronounced emphatically and the sound is prolonged.

3   Japanese words are pronounced much more evenly than English words, without as much stress or intonation. In English, we might say *kimono* or *yokohama* but in Japanese each syllable is said with about the same weight.

Konnichiwa!

saying hello and goodbye

introducing yourself

getting to know people

Nihon de wa ... *In Japan ...*

people bow to each other not only when they are meeting for the very first time, but also when they greet someone they know and when they say goodbye. A deep bow shows a greater degree of courtesy than a shallow one, so a department store employee, for example, would bow deeply while a customer would only incline the head and shoulders in return.

When greeting foreigners, Japanese people often shake hands instead of bowing.

Saying hello

1 **1•02** Listen to these key phrases.

Ohayō gozaimasu.	Good morning.
Ohayō.	Morning!
Konnichiwa.	Hello./Good afternoon.
Konbanwa.	Good evening.
(Yamada)-san	Mr, Mrs, Ms (Yamada)

2 **1•03** It's early in the day. Listen as Yamada-san greets three people arriving at the office. Tick the greeting she uses for each person.

	ohayō	ohayō gozaimasu
Ogawa-san		
Itō-san		
Ikeda-san		

Ohayō gozaimasu

Nihongo de wa … *In Japanese …*

people give their family name followed by their first name.
Ms Yamada, whose first name is Hiroko, would give her name as
Yamada Hiroko, although when speaking English she might follow
the English order.

---

3 **1•04** From late morning until early evening, Yamada-san uses a different greeting. Before you listen to the audio, decide which phrase you think she will use.

4 **1•05** Now listen as Yamada-san greets three people. What time of day is it?

	morning	afternoon	evening
Komatsu-san			
Kimura-san			
Nishimura-san			

... and goodbye

5   **1•06** Listen to these key phrases.

Shitsurei shimasu.	Please excuse me./Goodbye.
Sayōnara.	Goodbye.
Oyasumi nasai.	Goodnight. (at bedtime)

6   **1•07** It's at the end of the day. Listen to Yamada-san saying goodbye as she leaves the office. How many times do you hear **sayōnara**, and how many times do you hear **shitsurei shimasu**?

Nihongo de wa ...

Shitsurei shimasu means *Sorry, please excuse me*. But it is also a common and respectful way of saying goodbye. Note that the first **i** is hardly sounded, so you hear **sh'-tsu-re-i**.

7   **1•08** Yamada-san is saying goodnight to her parents before going to bed. Men often use slightly less formal phrases than women. What is the difference in the way her mother and her father wish her goodnight?

Mother ....   *Father* ....

8   Now try the following. How would you:

- greet a colleague formally in the morning?
- say goodbye after lunch?
- greet a friend in the evening?
- say goodnight?

Introducing yourself

1 **1•09** Listen to these key phrases.

(Watashi wa) … desu.	I'm …
Hajimemashite.	How do you do?
Dōzo yoroshiku.	Pleased to meet you.

Watashi wa (*I*) is often omitted.

2 **1•10** A hotel receptionist checks the names of several people as they arrive for a conference. Number the names in the order you hear them. Listen out for Ikeda-san saying **hai**. What do you think it means?

.... Ikeda Haruo   .... Suzuki Midori
.... Ogawa Akiko   .... Hashimoto Tarō

Nihongo de wa …

the word **san** is used after names as a term of respect, and can be used with family names or first names. The same word is used for men and women, married or unmarried. But remember that it is used only as a term of respect to other people, so you should never use it when giving your own name.

---

3 **1•11** Ikeda-san and Ogawa-san meet for the first time, and introduce themselves as they wait for the conference to begin. Number the key phrases above in the order you hear them.

4 **1•12** Listen as the delegates introduce themselves to the rest of the group. It's your turn after Ms Suzuki.

Suzuki-san Hajimemashite. Suzuki Midori desu. Dōzo yoroshiku.

You ....

... and getting to know people

5 **1•13** Listen to these key phrases.

Nishimura-san desu ka.	Are you Mr Nishimura?
Hai, sō desu.	Yes, that's right.
Shitsurei desu ga ...	Excuse me, but ...
O-namae wa?	What's your name?

6 **1•14** The receptionist is expecting either Kimura-san or Nishimura-san. Listen to their conversation – who is it? And what do you think **iie** means?

Nihongo de wa ...

to turn a statement into a question, simply add **ka** to the end. There is no need for a question mark.

Ogawa-san desu.	*She's Ms Ogawa.*
Ogawa-san desu ka.	*Is she Ms Ogawa?*
Sō desu.	*That's right.*
Sō desu ka.	*Is that right?/Really?*

Desu can mean *I am*, *he/she is* and *we/you/they are*. The meaning is usually clear from the context. It always comes at the end of the sentence, except in questions, where it is followed by **ka**. **G1**

---

7 **1•15** Yamada-san is working on the reception desk at her company when a visitor arrives. Listen and fill the gaps below.

Visitor	.... **gozaimasu.**
Yamada-san	.... **gozaimasu.** .... **desu ga, o-namae wa?**
Visitor	**Hashimoto desu.**
Yamada-san	**Hashimoto-**............. **desu ka.**
Visitor	**Hai,** .... **desu.**

san
ohayō
sō
ohayō
shitsurei

put it all together

1   Match the English with the Japanese.

a	Yes, that's right.	Hajimemashite.
b	Pleased to meet you.	Ohayō gozaimasu.
c	How do you do?	Konbanwa.
d	Good night.	Shitsurei shimasu.
e	Excuse me.	Hai, sō desu.
f	Really?	O-namae wa?
g	Good evening.	Sō desu ka.
h	Good morning.	Dōzo yoroshiku.
i	What's your name?	Oyasumi nasai.

2   What could these people be saying to each other?

a

b

c

3   The following names are all in this unit. Try saying them out loud, then listen to the audio to check your pronunciation. Notice how all syllables have equal stress, and how the vowel sounds (a, e, i, o, u) are clearly sounded.

women	men
Yamada Hiroko	Ikeda Haruo
Suzuki Midori	Hashimoto Tarō
Ogawa Akiko	

now you're talking!

1 **1•16** Imagine you're Steve Wilson, staying at a small hotel in Tokyo. The receptionist checks your name on her list as you're about to go on a bus tour one morning.

- ◆ Greet the receptionist.
- ● **Ohayō gozaimasu. Shitsurei desu ga, o-namae wa?**
- ◆ Tell her your name.
- ● **Wilson-san desu ka.**
- ◆ Say *Yes, that's right*.

2 **1•17** As you wait at the hotel door for the tour bus to arrive, you're talking to another guest and think you see a famous Japanese actress, Keiko Sakai.

- ◆ Ask if that's Ms Sakai.
- ● **Hai, sō desu. Sakai Keiko-san desu.**
- ◆ Say *Oh really?*

3 **1•18** On the bus, you sit next to Kimura-san, who introduces herself.

- ● **Hajimemashite. Kimura Akiko desu. Dōzo yoroshiku.**
- ◆ Introduce yourself, and say you're pleased to meet her.

4 **1•19** The tour has finished, and you return to your hotel.

- ◆ Say goodbye to Ms Kimura.
- ● **Shitsurei shimasu.**

5 **1•20** When you arrive back at the hotel in the evening, you meet an acquaintance, Itō-san, in the bar.

- ◆ Greet Itō-san.
- ● **Konbanwa.**
- ◆ At the end of the evening, say goodnight.

quiz

1 When would you say **konnichiwa**?
2 Would you say **oyasumi nasai** in the morning?
3 If someone asks you **O-namae wa**? what do you answer?
4 How would you greet someone in the evening?
5 What do you add to **ohayō** to make it more polite?
6 Which part of this sentence is it possible to leave out and still be correct? **Watashi wa Tanaka Keiko desu**.
7 Would you use **shitsurei shimasu** to say *hello* or *goodbye*?
8 When do you say **hajimemashite**?
9 Are **Ikeda**, **Sakai** and **Yamada** first names or family names?
10 Is **Tanaka-san desu ka** a statement or a question?

Now check whether you can ...

- greet someone correctly in the morning, during the day and in the evening
- say goodbye in two different ways
- say goodnight
- greet someone you meet for the first time
- give your name
- ask someone's name

When you practise your Japanese, make sure you say the words and phrases out loud. You'll notice that Japanese doesn't have such a strong up and down rhythm as English so, using the audio, try to imitate not only the pronunciation of each word but also the rhythm and intonation of the whole sentence or question. Listen to the audio as often as you can. The more you listen the more comfortable you'll become with the language.

O-kuni wa?

talking about your nationality

... and where you're from

saying what you do for a living

giving your phone number

Nihon de wa ...

people are always delighted to hear their language being spoken, so it's well worth learning how to say a little about yourself and to ask simple questions so you can make conversation. You'll find that people rarely use the equivalent of *you* but rather use a person's name even when talking directly to that person.

When talking about work, people often use very general terms rather than giving their specific job. So they may say they are **kaishain** *an office worker*, or **ginkōin** *a bank worker* or even simply **sarariiman** *a salaried worker*.

Talking about your nationality

1 **1•21** Listen to these key phrases.

... desu ka	Are you ...?
Amerika-jin desu ka.	Are you American?
Iie, Amerika-jin ja arimasen.	No, I'm not American.
Igirisu-jin desu.	I'm English/British.
Arigatō.	Thank you.
Arigatō gozaimasu.	Thank you very much. (formal)

2 **1•22** Hayashi-san is researching numbers of American visitors to Kyoto for a travel company. Tick the nationalities as you hear them.

	Igirisu-jin	Amerika-jin	Ōsutoraria-jin
visitor 1			
visitor 2			
visitor 3			

Nihongo de wa ...

ja arimasen is the negative of **desu**, so it means *am not* or *isn't/aren't*. You might also hear the more formal **dewa arimasen**. **G3**

---

3 **1•23** You give your nationality by adding **-jin** *person* to the name of your country. Can you work out what these countries are and then how you would say the nationality in Japanese? Finally, listen to the audio for the pronunciation.

Nihon	**Igirisu**	**Amerika**	**Sukottorando**
Uēruzu	**Ōsutoraria**	**Airurando**	**Kanada**

4 How would you reply if someone asked you **Amerika-jin desu ka**?

... and where you're from

5 **1•24** Listen to these key phrases.

O-kuni wa dochira desu ka.   Which country are you from?
dochira   where?
Igirisu desu.   I'm from England.

6 **1•25** Listen as Hayashi-san continues with her survey and then fill in the gaps.

Hayashi-san   **Shitsurei desu ga, ...** wa dochira desu ka.

Sue   **..............................** desu.

Hayashi-san   **Sō desu ka. Rondon ....**

Sue   **Iie, Rondon .... Manchesutā desu.**

Nihongo de wa ...

the word **wa** has no equivalent in English, but it comes at the end of a word or phrase to indicate it is the topic under discussion.

O-kuni wa Furansu desu ka.   *Your country – is it France?*
         i.e. *Are you from France?*

Yamada-san wa Nihon-jin desu.   *Yamada-san – she is Japanese.*

                                          G6

---

7 Is Mr Jones saying he is or isn't from California?

Kariforunia ja arimasen

Saying what you do for a living

1 **1•26** Listen to these key phrases.

O-shigoto wa?	What do you do?
Gakusei desu ka.	Are you a student?
Hashimoto-san mo gakusei desu ka.	Are you a student too, Mr Hashimoto?
Kaisha wa Tōkyō desu.	(My) company is in Tokyo.
Kimura-san wa?	How about you, Ms Kimura?

2 **1•27** Ikeda-san is chatting to some people. Listen, and then match the names to the occupations in the box.

Ogawa-san ....

Hashimoto-san ....

Kimura-san ....

> **shufu** *housewife*
> **kaishain** *office worker*
> **enjinia** *engineer*
> **gakusei** *student*
> **sensei** *teacher*
> **isha** *doctor*

Nihongo de wa ...

o- is added to the beginning of some words to show politeness to others (**o-namae, o-shigoto**) so don't use it when talking about your own name, job etc.

Questions are often left unfinished if the meaning is obvious.
O-shigoto wa? *Your job?* **O-kuni wa?** *Your country?*
O-namae wa? *Your name?*

G13

---

3 How would you describe Mike Green? Example: **Hashimoto-san wa Nihon-jin desu. Kaishain desu. Kaisha wa Ōsaka desu.**

Name: HASHIMOTO, Tarō
Nationality: Japanese
Occupation: office worker
Location: Ōsaka

Name: GREEN, Mike
Nationality: British
Occupation: engineer
Location: London

Can you now describe a friend?

Giving your phone number

1 **1•28** Listen to the numbers 0 to 10 and practise saying them aloud.

0	*1*	*2*	*3*	*4*	*5*
rei, zero	**ichi**	**ni**	**san**	**yon**	**go**

6	*7*	*8*	*9*	*10*
roku	**nana**	**hachi**	**kyū**	**jū**

2 **1•29** Hayashi-san asks the office extension numbers (**nai-sen bangō**) of four work colleagues. Try saying the numbers, then listen to the audio to check.

 Yamada 348 Ogawa 926 Tanaka 815 Ishii 577

Nihongo de wa ...

no after a word shows possession or belonging: **Watashi no** *my* **Yamada-san no** *Yamada-san's*, **kaisha no** *the company's*. **G8**

---

3 **1•30** Listen to these key phrases, all about **denwa bangō** *phone numbers*.

Watashi no denwa bangō wa ... desu.	My phone number is ...
Denwa bangō wa nan-ban desu ka.	What's your phone number?
kaisha no denwa bangō	company's phone number

4 **1•31** Ikeda-san checks the phone numbers of two tourists. Check the numbers with him and circle any mistakes you find. Listen for the dash in between the numbers, voiced as **no**.

 Hirano-san 03—4823—3311 Matsumoto-san 0473—63—9445

Now practise saying your own **denwa bangō** and then the numbers of friends and family.

put it all together

1   Which answer best fits the question?

a	Igirisu-jin desu ka.	Watashi wa shufu desu.
b	Shitsurei desu ga, o-kuni wa?	Iie, Airurando-jin desu.
c	Tanaka-san wa gakusei desu ka.	416-9227 desu.
d	O-shigoto wa?	Igirisu desu.
e	Denwa bangō wa nan-ban desu ka.	Iie, kaishain desu.

2   Look at Ikeda-san's name card. What short questions could you ask to get the information indicated?

> Kiku Engineering Ltd.
> Haruo Ikeda ← a
> Engineer
> 5-5-1 Kiku, Chuo-ku, Tokyo 100, Japan ← c
> Tel (03) 3352-6528

b →

d →

3   Ikeda-san gets talking to Tom, a guest in the hotel where he's working. Put these lines into the correct order to make a conversation.

c Hai, sō desu. Ikeda-san wa?

a Sō desu ka. Rondon desu ka.

b Shitsurei desu ga, o-kuni wa Amerika desu ka.

e Iie, kaisha wa Tōkyō desu.

d Iie, Amerika ja arimasen. Igirisu desu.

f Kaisha mo Yokohama desu ka.

g Watashi wa Yokohama desu.

now you're talking!

1 **1•32** Imagine you're on holiday in Kyoto, and someone starts a conversation with you by asking if you're American. You'll need to know how to:

◆ say you're not American.
◆ say you're English, not from London but from York.
◆ say yes, you're a student.

2 **1•33** Now imagine you are Andrew Fairlie and play his part in the conversation.

● **Shitsurei desu ga, o-kuni wa dochira desu ka.**
◆ *You*
● **Sō desu ka. Rondon desu ka.**
◆ *You*
● **Sō desu ka. Watashi wa Hashimoto desu. O-namae wa?**

Occupation: Engineer
Nationality: English
Home Town: London

◆ *You*
● **Fairlie-san, o-shigoto wa?**
◆ *You*
◆ **Watashi desu ka. Watashi wa isha desu.**

3 **1•34** You're checking into a small hotel and the receptionist asks you for some personal details to fill in the registration form.

● **Shitsurei desu ga, o-namae wa?**
◆ *You*
● **O-kuni wa?**
◆ *You*
● **O-shigoto wa?**
◆ *You*
● **O-denwa bangō wa?**
◆ *You*
● **Hai, arigatō gozaimasu.**

quiz

1 What word do you add to the end of a country name to give a nationality?

2 Which word implies the meaning *my job* – **shigoto** or **o-shigoto**?

3 Cross out the number which doesn't fit the sequence:
   san yon go ichi roku

4 Which of the following is the odd one out?
   Furansu Pari Itaria Sukottorando

5 What do you add to **watashi** to make a phrase meaning *my*?

6 How would someone ask you your nationality?

7 Which word turns a sentence into a question, **wa** or **ka**?

8 Is a **shufu** male or female?

9 How would you tell someone you're not a student?

10 If you were asked **Kaisha no denwa bangō wa nan-ban desu ka**, what information would you give?

Now check whether you can ...

- say what nationality you are
- say where you're from
- say what you do for a living
- give your phone number
- ask others for this information

There are many tricks you can use to remember new words and phrases. You could try listing them in a notebook with different pages for different kinds of words, or put them on sticky labels in places where you can't fail to notice them. You could record them on to your own audio, or you could get someone else to test you – it doesn't have to be a Japanese speaker.

Go-shōkai shimasu

meeting friends

introducing another person

talking about other people

... and asking their age

Nihon de wa ...

most people, particularly those in business, carry name cards, or **meishi**, and exchange them when being introduced for the first time. For professional people, the fact that the name card shows the person's name, company and hierarchy within that company helps to establish seniority. For everyone, the cards act as a valuable aid in remembering names and other details about the person. The **meishi** should be treated with respect, and carefully placed in a wallet after being scrutinised, rather than carelessly put into a pocket without a glance. If you're going to Japan, you might consider having some name cards printed.

Meeting friends

1 **1•35** Listen to these key phrases.

Shibaraku desu ne.	It's been a long time, hasn't it!
genki	well, healthy
O-genki desu ka.	Are you well?
Hai, o-kage sama de.	Yes, thank you for asking.
Kyō wa iya-na tenki desu ne.	Horrible weather today, isn't it!
kyō	today

2 **1•36** At a conference, Ogawa-san meets up with an old friend, Honda-san. Tick the key phrases as you hear them.

> **Nihongo de wa ...**
>
> people only use **o-genki desu ka** when they haven't seen one another for some time. It's not used in the same way as the English *How are you?*
>
> **Ne**, added to the end of a sentence, makes it into an exclamation – it's the equivalent of *isn't it?/aren't they?/didn't you?*
> **Ii tenki desu ne.** *Nice weather, isn't it?*

3 **1•37** People often comment about the weather as a casual greeting. Listen to three short snatches of conversation as people greet each other in the street, and match the dialogues *a* to *c* with the appropriate picture.

1  2  3

> **atsui** *hot*
> **samui** *cold*
> **mushiatsui** *hot and humid*

... and introducing another person

4   **1•38** Listen to these key phrases.

Go-shōkai shimasu.	Let me introduce you.
Kochira wa Tōkyō Ginkō	This is Ms Honda of Tokyo Bank.
no Honda-san desu.	
kochira	this, this person (formal)

Nihongo de wa ...

no can show belonging in a wider sense than just possession.
People often introduce themselves in terms of their company
Tōkyō Ginkō no Honda desu *I'm Honda, of Tokyo Bank*, or country
Amerika no James desu *I'm James, from America*.   **G8**

---

5   **1•39** Ogawa-san is chatting to Honda-san before the conference
begins, when a business acquaintance, Mori-san, joins them. Listen as
Ogawa-san introduces him to Honda-san.

6   **1•40** Yamada-san chats to a friend as her English teacher (**Eigo no
sensei**), Mr James, approaches. Listen and fill in the gaps.

Yamada-san	**A, sensei, konnichiwa.**
Mr James	**Konnichiwa. Kyō wa samui ....**
Yamada-san	**Sō desu ne. Go-shōkai .... Sensei,**
	.... Yamaguchi-san desu.
Yamaguchi-san	**Yamaguchi desu. Dōzo yoroshiku.**
Mr James	**James desu. Dōzo yoroshiku.**

Did you notice how Yamada-san referred to her teacher, not with **san**,
but with the title **sensei**?

Talking about other people

1   **1•41** Listen to these key phrases.

Kochira wa okusan desu ka.	Is this your wife?
Okusan mo sensei desu ka.	Is your wife a teacher too?
Hai, kanai mo sensei desu.	Yes, my wife's a teacher too.

Nihongo de wa ...

the language you use shows if you're talking about someone within your own close group (family, company colleagues, close friends) or someone from outside that group:

go-shujin *your husband*   **shujin** *my husband*
okusan *your wife*   **kanai** *my wife*
o-tomodachi *your friend*   **tomodachi** *my friend*   **G13**

---

2   **1•42** James-sensei is just back from holiday, and shows some holiday photos to Yamada-san. Listen and fill in the gaps below.

Yamada-san	**Kochira wa .... desu ka.**
Mr James	**Hai, sō desu. .... desu.**
Yamada-san	**Shitsurei desu ga, okusan mo sensei desu ka.**
Mr James	**Hai, sō desu. .... Eigo no sensei desu.**

3   **1•43** Now listen to someone who is interested in getting to know Yamada-san's friend better. He comes over to speak to Yamada-san after her friend has left. What question does he ask first?

... and asking their age

4 **1•44** Look at the following numbers. Can you work out how to say 15 to 19? Check with the audio.

10	11	12	13	14
jū	jū-ichi	jū-ni	jū-san	jū-yon

15	16	17	18	19
....	....	....	....	....

5 **1•45** Listen to some more numbers and try to find the patterns. What is the next number in each case?

20	30	40	50	60	70
ni-jū	san-jū	yon-jū	go-jū	roku-jū	....

65	66	67	68	69
roku-jū go	roku-jū roku	roku-jū nana	roku-jū hachi	....

6 **1•46** Listen to the key phrases.

O-ikutsu desu ka.   How old is she?
Tanaka-san wa 35-sai desu.   Tanaka-san is 35.
Gārufrendo wa wakai desu ne.   His girlfriend is young, isn't she?

Nihongo de wa ...

to say how old someone is, just add **-sai** to the number, with the following exceptions: *1*, *8* and *10 years old* become **issai**, **hassai** and **jussai**. There is a special word for *20 years old* (when someone legally becomes an adult) – **hatachi**.

---

7 **1•47** Listen to two people talking as they see one of their colleagues with someone who looks very young, then answer the questions.

a Who is Tanaka-san with?   **b** About how old is she?
c How old is Tanaka-san?

put it **all together**

1   Can you find four words to describe the weather in this word square, either horizontally or vertically?

T	B	U	S	S	T	R	O	S	M
R	A	A	T	A	T	A	K	A	I
N	T	A	I	M	S	H	P	N	Y
U	S	U	Z	U	S	H	I	I	A
R	U	Z	K	I	T	R	M	S	N
K	I	I	S	U	T	I	K	M	A

2   Match up the two halves of the sentences.

a	**Kochira wa**	sensei desu.
b	**Okusan wa**	iya-na tenki desu ne.
c	**Kanai no namae wa**	Yamaha no Saitō-san desu.
d	**Kyō wa**	o-genki desu ka.
e	**Watashi mo**	Keiko desu.

3   How would you describe this friend of yours?

Name: *Ms Ogawa* ....

Age: *19* ....

Occupation: *Student* ....

now you're **talking!**

1 **1•48** Imagine you're chatting to someone in your hotel as she shows you some family photos.

- ◆ Ask if this picture is of her husband.
- ● **Hai, sō desu.**
- ◆ Ask what her husband's job is.
- ● **Kaishain desu.**
- ◆ Ask how old he is.
- ● **47-sai desu.**
- ◆ Comment on how young he looks.

2 **1•49** Another hotel guest you first met some time ago walks past. His name is Suzuki-san and he works for Yamaha.

- ◆ Say *hello*, and mention that it's a while since you last met.
- ● **Sō desu ne.**
- ◆ Ask him if he's well.
- ● **Hai, o-kage sama de. Genki desu.**
- ◆ Suzuki-san is obviously suffering in the heat. Comment that today is very humid.
- ● **Sō desu ne. Iya-na tenki desu ne.**
- ◆ Introduce Suzuki-san to your other friend, mentioning his company.
- ● **Suzuki desu. Dōzo yoroshiku.**

3 **1•50** You're chatting to a man by the hotel pool.

- ◆ Comment on how hot it is today.
- ● **Sō desu ne. Atsui desu ne.**
- ◆ He waves to a woman in the pool. Ask if it's his wife.
- ● **Iie, sō ja arimasen. Gārufurendo desu.**

quiz

1 Would you introduce a close friend with **kochira wa ...**?
2 If you are told that someone is **san-jussai**, is she 3, 13 or 30 years old?
3 Would you put a coat on if the weather were **atsui**?
4 Would you be pleased or sorry if a friend said she was **genki**?
5 How would you address Ms Yamashita, who is a teacher?
6 Can you say how old you are in Japanese?
7 Would you say **shibaraku desu ne** to someone you last met yesterday?
8 What would someone be about to do if they said **go-shōkai shimasu**?

Now check whether you can ...

- introduce someone from a different company
- use numbers up to 99
- talk about your spouse
- ask about age, and give your own age
- greet someone you haven't seen for a long time
- comment on the weather

Review your progress frequently. You could keep a diary of your learning and set yourself firm objectives, for example to complete a unit by a particular date. The key to successful learning is to work steadily and regularly – a short fifteen-minute session, every day, is far more effective than one long session, once a week.

Kōhii o kudasai

ordering a drink in a coffee shop

offering someone a drink

... and accepting or refusing

Nihon de wa ...

kissaten *coffee shops* are popular places for people to gather. The coffee may be expensive but you can sit there all day, reading the paper, chatting to friends or even having a meeting. If you want something stronger to drink in the evening, then go to an **izakaya**, where you can get snacks as well as beer (**biiru**) and **sake** *rice wine*.

In the **kissaten**, **izakaya** or restaurant, you will get a glass of ice-cold water and an **oshibori** *moist towel* to refresh yourself as you look at the menu. And wherever you go, you'll be greeted with a friendly **Irasshaimase!** *Welcome!* as you enter.

Ordering a drink

1 **1•51** Listen to these key phrases.

Sumimasen.	Excuse me!
Nani ni nasaimasu ka.	What will you have? (formal)
Kōhii o kudasai.	A coffee, please.
Chiizu sando	A cheese sandwich
… to kōra o kudasai.	… and a coke, please.

2 **1•52** Listen as Yamada-san orders a snack and something to drink in a coffee shop. What does she order first?

Nihongo de wa ...

... **o kudasai** is used when you want someone to give you something, so it's similar to *I'd like* ... or *Please could I have* ... The little word **o** identifies the item you want by coming directly after it.

3 Many of the words for items of food and drink in coffee shops have been taken from English, although of course the pronunciation has changed. Can you guess what these are?

a kōhii	f hanbāgā
b orenji jūsu	g aisu kuriimu
c remon jūsu	h hamu sando
d miruku	i chiizukēki
e kokoa	j tōsuto

4 **1•53** Listen as Yamada-san's friends arrive in the coffee shop and order drinks and snacks. Check off the items on the menu above as you hear them.

... in a coffee shop

5   **1•54** Listen to these key phrases.

Ja, kore o kudasai.	Well, I'll have this, please.
Remon tii o futatsu.	Two lemon teas.

6   **1•55** If you don't know the word for something, you can point to the object and ask for **kore** *this one*, **sore** *that one* or **are** *that one over there*. Listen to someone in the **kissaten** looking at pastries and asking what they all are. Which one does she decide to have?

Nihongo de wa ...

there are various numbering systems, depending on the objects you are counting – rather like the English *bar of chocolate*, *piece of paper*. Here are the first five numbers of the most commonly used system, meaning *one thing*, *two things* etc:

1	*2*	*3*	*4*	*5*	
hitotsu	futatsu	mittsu	yottsu	itsutsu	**G11**

---

7   **1•56** Listen to the family at the next table giving their order and fill in the gaps. How many of each item do they order?

Waitress	**Nani ni nasaimasu ka.**
Father	**Hamu sando …………… remon tii o kudasai.**
Mother	**Watashi mo remon tii. Remon tii to aisu kuriimu …………… kudasai.**
Daughter	**…………… aisu kuriimu to kōra o kudasai.**
Waitress	**Hai. Remon tii o ……………, hamu sando o hitotsu, aisu kuriimu o futatsu, kōra o …………… desu ne.**
Mother	**Hai, sō desu.**

Offering someone a drink

1   **1•57** Listen to these key phrases.

Dōzo.	Here you are.
O-cha o dōzo.	Here's some green tea.
Mō sukoshi ikaga desu ka.	Would you like a little more?
Kōhii wa ikaga desu ka.	(Would you like) coffee?
Hai, onegai shimasu.	Yes, please.
Iie, kekkō desu.	No, thank you./No, this is fine.

2   **1•58** O-cha *green tea* is often served to visitors in the office or home. Listen as a visitor arrives at Kiku Engineering to see Ikeda-san and tick the key phrases you hear.

Does he have more than one cup of **o-cha**?

3   **1•59** Listen to Yamada-san visiting a friend in the evening. Which of these did her friend offer her? Did she accept?

tea	green tea	coffee
sugar	milk	cream

Nihongo de wa ...

there are several ways of saying *please*.
(Kōhii) o kudasai is a polite way of saying *Please give me (some coffee)*, used when asking for an object.
Onegai shimasu is a way of saying *Please do that*, used when asking someone to do something for you.

4   How would you ask someone if they would like:
- a coffee?
- a tea?
- a little more?

... and accepting or refusing

5   **1•60** Listen to these key phrases.

Kanpai!	Cheers!
Itadakimasu.	(set phrase said before eating or drinking)
Oishii desu.	It's good/tasty.
O-kanjō o onegai shimasu.	The bill, please.
Gochisō sama deshita.	(set phrase of general thanks said after a meal)

6   **1•61** Ikeda-san is in an **izakaya** after work and orders **biiru** *a beer* while waiting for a colleague, Fujie-san. Listen to the conversation as Fujie-san arrives, then fill in the appropriate set phrases.

Ikeda-san **Fujie-san, konbanwa. Biiru wa ikaga desu ka.**
Fujie-san **Hai, onegai shimasu. Arigatō.**
Ikeda-san ....!
Fujie-san ....!
Ikeda-san .... ne!

7   **1•62** They order **yakitori** (small pieces of barbecued chicken). Number the phrases below in the order you think they will appear, then listen to the conversation to check.

mō sukoshi ....   o-kanjō o onegai shimasu ....
kekkō desu ....   itadakimasu ....
gochisō sama deshita ....   oishii desu ne....................

Did Fujie-san want some **o-sake** after the beer?

Nihongo de wa ...

Arigatō gozaimashita is the past tense of **Arigatō gozaimasu** and is used to say a polite thank you for something which has already been done or completed. When you leave a restaurant, the staff will say **Arigatō gozaimashita** *Thank you for your custom*. Another, more informal, way of saying *Thanks* to someone is **Dōmo**.

put it all together

1   Choose the correct response

a Mō sukoshi ikaga desu ka.	1 Hai, sō desu.
	2 Iie, kekkō desu.
b Kōhii o dōzo.	1 Arigatō.
	2 Onegai shimasu.
c Nani ni nasaimasu ka.	1 Itadakimasu.
	2 Yakitori o kudasai.

2   Now put these words in the correct order.
   a   yottsu / kōcha / kudasai / o
   b   kudasai / kōhii / tōsuto / to / o
   c   oishii / yakitori / wa / desu
   d   kore / desu / wa / appuru pai

3   Look at this waiter's order pad. What did each customer order?

   a   kōhii – 2, chiizukēki – 1
   b   kōcha – 3, hamu sando – 2
   c   kōra – 4, aisu kuriimu – 3

4   1•63 The following words from this unit all have double letters. Read them out loud, making sure you pronounce the double letters by holding them for twice as long as a single letter. Listen to the pronunciation on the audio.

   mi<u>tt</u>su   yo<u>tt</u>su   ke<u>kk</u>ō   ki<u>ss</u>aten   a<u>pp</u>uru pai

now you're talking!

1 **1•64** Imagine you're in a **kissaten** in Tokyo with a friend. You're looking at the menu and getting ready to order.

   ◆ You call the waitress.
   ● **Hai, nani ni nasaimasu ka.**
   ◆ You order two iced coffees and a cheese sandwich.

For the following conversations, make sure you know the words and phrases, then take your cue from the audio.

2 **1•65** You've arrived at Kiku Engineering where you have an appointment.

   ◆ You're offered coffee.
   ◆ You accept and are offered cream.
   ◆ Say you don't want cream.

3 **1•66** Later in the day you plan to meet a friend in an **izakaya** for a drink and a snack; you arrive early.

   ◆ Order a beer.
   ◆ When your drink arrives thank the barman.

Kanpai!

4 **1•67** Your friend has arrived.

   ◆ Ask if he'd like some beer and pour it for him, say *Here you are*. Say *Cheers!*
   ◆ When the **yakitori** arrives, thank the barman and say the appropriate phrase before you eat.
   ◆ As you get ready to leave the bar, ask the barman for the bill.
   ◆ When you get up to leave, use the set phrase to thank the barman for the food and snacks.

quiz

1 Who would say **irasshaimase** to you, and when?

2 What is **sake** (or more politely, **o-sake**)?

3 How would you order two coffees and an ice cream?

4 When would you say **gochisō sama deshita**?

5 What is the set expression you use before eating or drinking?

6 What would you say to attract someone's attention?

7 What is the Japanese for *Cheers!*?

8 If you want to drink beer or **sake** in the evening, would you go to an **izakaya** or a **kissaten**?

9 If you didn't know the name of something, how would you say *I'll have that, please*?

10 If someone tasted your cooking and said it was **oishii**, would you be pleased?

Now check whether you can ...

- order a drink and snack
- offer someone a drink
- accept when someone offers you a drink
  ... or refuse politely
- use the appropriate polite expressions before eating and drinking
- ask for something by pointing to it
- count items up to five

As so many English words have been adopted into Japanese (see *Wordpower*, page 133), you could always try using English with Japanese pronunciation when you don't know a particular word. As a foreigner, you'll not offend anyone if you get something wrong; even if it doesn't turn out to be completely correct Japanese, the chances are that you will be understood – in tight spots this can be a very successful strategy.

Chekkupointo 1

1   **1•68** Listen to a student doing some research among tourists in Kyoto, then choose the right information. Listen out for her first question:

Shigoto desu ka. Yasumi desu ka.   *Are you here for work or are you on holiday?*

a   **Shigoto desu ka.**   yasumi/shigoto desu
    Yasumi desu ka.
b   **Ann-san no kuni wa?**   Igirisu/Amerika desu
c   **Tomodachi no kuni wa?**   Igirisu/Amerika desu
d   **Ann-san wa?**   ginkōin/kaishain desu

2   **1•69** While on the train, you overhear two students getting to know one another. Listen to their conversation and fill in the missing details.

Name	Nationality	Age	Student where?
Takeshi Saito	Japanese		
Jenny Davies			

3   **1•70** Takeshi and Jenny buy some drinks and snacks when the drinks trolley comes down the train. What do they each have?

4   **1•71** Practise saying the Japanese for these items of food and drink and then check your pronunciation with the audio.

chiizu   hamu   aisu kuriimu   tomato

hanbāgā   kēki   wain   banana

5 **1•72** Listen to a phone operator giving the dialling codes for various countries and write in the missing numbers.

Can you guess what the countries are?

Burajiru	00 55	Oranda	00 ....
Indo	00	Suēden	00 ....
Mekishiko	00	Tai	00 ....
Nepāru	00	Maruta	00 ....

A good way to practise low numbers is to throw two dice and say out loud all the possible number combinations:

ichi
go
jū-go
go-jū ichi

6 Choose the right expression for the following situations.

a You're introduced to someone.
b You meet someone you haven't seen for a while.
c You're about to drink some beer with friends.
d You're about to begin a meal.
e Saying goodbye with the phrase *excuse me*.
f You're given something.
g You greet someone in the evening.

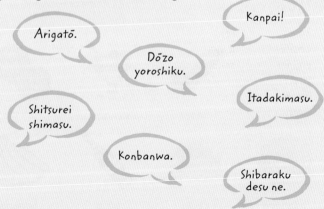

Kanpai!

Arigatō.

Dōzo yoroshiku.

Itadakimasu.

Shitsurei shimasu.

Konbanwa.

Shibaraku desu ne.

7   A Japanese colleague has asked you to help his son fill in an
    application form for an English course in London. What are the
    questions you would need to ask him before you could fill in the
    missing entries?

Name: ....

Address: 6-9-26 kitazawa, Minato-ku Tōkyō 137

Phone no.: ....

Age: ....

Nationality: Japanese ....

Occupation: ....

a   ....
b   ....
c   ....
d   ....

8   These are the Japanese characters for the numbers 1, 2, 3 and 4, which
    have appeared at the top of the first four units. Can you put them in
    the correct order?

四	二	一	三
a	b	c	d

9   Which is the odd one out in these groups of words?

a	kore	rei	sore	are
b	dochira	ikaga	nan-ban	shufu
c	enjinia	sensei	shigoto	sarariiman
d	kirai	shujin	okusan	kanai
e	hitotsu	futatsu	itsutsu	atsui
f	nani	hachi	san	kyū

10 Fill in the gaps to complete the crossword.

Across

1 O-cha wa .... desu ka.

4 Iie, watashi wa gakusei ja ....

6 Kōhii o hitotsu .... kōra o futatsu kudasai.

7 Yamada-.......... wa o-ikutsu desu ka.

9 .... wa atsui desu ne!

10 Amerika-................. desu ka.

Down

1 .... tenki desu ne.

2 Dōmo ....

3 .... bangō wa nan-ban desu ka.

5 .... wa appuru pai desu ka.

7 Ikura desu ka. .... en desu.

8 Kyō wa .... -yobi desu ka.

9 O-namae wa nan desu ....

Tōkyō eki wa doko desu ka

asking where something is

asking for help to understand

talking about where you live and work

Nihon de wa ...

addresses are based on district areas, with numbered blocks within those areas. Most streets, except the major thoroughfares, don't have names, and often buildings are not numbered consecutively, so it can be difficult to find a house or office building just from the address!

People often ask the way at one of the many local **kōban** *police box*. **Kōban** can be found at most major intersections and near stations, and the police are used to helping visitors to their area with directions.

Asking where something is

1 **1•73** Listen to these key phrases.

Yūbinkyoku wa koko desu.	The post office is here.
Soko desu.	It's there.
Asoko desu.	It's over there.
Tōkyō eki wa doko desu ka.	Where's Tokyo station?
Mō ichido, onegai shimasu.	Could you repeat that, please?
Wakarimasen.	I don't know./I don't understand.

2 **1•74** Listen to two tourists as they look at a map of Tokyo. They're trying to find Mitsukoshi Department Store (**depāto**). Can you guess what a **hoteru** is?

Nihongo de wa ...

sumimasen *excuse me* is sometimes used instead of **arigatō** as a way of thanking someone when acknowledging a favour. It includes the nuance of apologising for having caused any bother.

---

3 **1•75** Listen to a tourist asking where the station is and complete their conversation.

Tourist	**Sumimasen. Tōkyō eki wa ....**
Passer-by 1	**Watashi mo ....**
Tourist	**Sō desu ka. Dōmo ....**
	Sumimasen. Tōkyō eki wa ....
Passer-by 2	**A, Tōkyō eki desu ka. ....**
Tourist	**Dōmo arigatō.**

4 **1•76** Listen as a lost tourist, looking for her hotel, stops at a **kōban** to ask a police officer the way. Where is her hotel?

... and asking for help to understand

5 **1•77** Listen to these key phrases.

Eki no ushiro desu	It's behind the station
Motto yukkuri, onegai shimasu	A little more slowly, please

Nihongo de wa ...

to describe where something is in relation to another place, the word order is as follows:

Kōban wa eki no mae desu.
The police box is in front of the station.
Kissaten wa ginkō no tonari desu.
The coffee shop is next to the bank.
Naka (in, inside), **ushiro** (behind), **mae** (in front of), **mukai** (opposite), **tonari** (next to), are all used in the same way.

6 Look at this map, and say if the following statements are true or false.

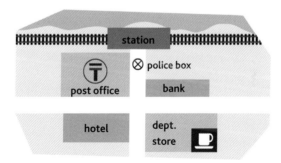

	true	false
a **Kōban wa eki no mae desu.**		
b **Ginkō wa depāto no ushiro desu.**		
c **Kissaten wa depāto no tonari desu.**		
d **Yūbinkyoku wa hoteru no mukai desu.**		

7 **1•78** Now listen to someone looking for the park (**kōen**). Where is it on the map?

Talking about where you live

1   **1•79** Listen to these key phrases.

O-sumai wa dochira desu ka.   Where do you live? (formal)
Rondon no chikaku desu.   It's near London.

2   **1•80** Ikeda-san is travelling to Kyoto on business and begins chatting to an English tourist on the train. Is she from London or Reading?

> **Nihongo de wa ...**
>
> **o-sumai** *house, home* and **dochira** *where?* are polite words used when talking to someone you don't know very well. In more informal situations, or when talking about someone who isn't present, you can use **uchi** and **doko** instead.
>
> **Tanaka san no uchi wa doko desu ka.**
> *Where's Tanaka-san's house?*

3   **1•81** Yamada-san's friend has just told her that she's moving home next weekend. Listen as Yamada-san asks about her **atarashii uchi** *new home*. Where is it?

Listen again. Can you guess what an **apāto** is?

4   **1•82** Now listen to another friend talking about where he lives and circle which of each pair below describes his home.

- in Yokohama/in Nakano
- near station/near park
- flat/house
- old/new

... and work

5 **1•83** Listen to these key phrases.

O-tsutome wa dochira desu ka.	Where do you work? (formal)
Iie, chigaimasu.	No, it's not/No, that's not correct.
Kono chikaku desu ka.	Is it near here?
Sono depāto no tonari desu.	It's next to that department store.
Ano biru desu.	It's that building over there.

6 **1•84** Ikeda-san bumps into an old friend and asks where she's working **ima** *now*. Is she far from her office right now?

> ## Nihongo de wa ...
>
> **kono** *this/these*, **sono** *that/those*, **ano** *that/those over there* and **dono** *which?* are always followed by a noun.
>
> In contrast, **kore**, **sore**, **are**, **dore** mean *this thing*, *that thing* etc, and so can stand alone.
>
> | | | |
> |---|---|---|
> | **Kono biru wa ginkō desu ka.** | *Is this building a bank?* | |
> | **Kore wa ginkō desu ka.** | *Is this a bank?* | **G14** |

7 **1•85** Listen to a young woman asking her friend about her new boyfriend, Takeshi-san. Are these statements true or false?

		true	false
a	Takeshi-san works in an office.		
b	His company is nearby.		
c	His office is in the department store.		

8 Can you say:

- where you live?
- what it's near?
- where you work? If you don't work, talk about a friend.

put it all together

1   Match the questions to the answers.

a	Kōban wa doko desu ka.	Yokohama desu.
b	Kōen wa eki no mae desu ka.	Hoteru wa ano biru desu.
c	Apāto wa dochira desu ka.	Iie, ushiro desu.
d	Hoteru wa dono biru desu ka.	Iie, chigaimasu. Yokohama desu.
e	Kaisha wa kono chikaku desu ka.	Eki no mae desu.

2   Put the words in order and match them to the situations below.

onegai / ichido / mō / shimasu
dochira / ka / desu / o-sumai / wa
biru / desu / ka / dono
depāto / naka / kissaten / no / wa / desu

a   You need to know where someone lives.
b   You confirm where the coffee shop is.
c   You didn't catch what someone said.
d   You're not quite sure which building someone is talking about.

3   Put these sentences in order to make a conversation between two friends chatting about an acquaintance, Tanaka-san.

a   Sono ginkō no tonari desu.
b   Kaisha desu ka. Sono biru desu.
c   Watashi mo wakarimasen.
d   Tanaka-san no uchi? Wakarimasen.
e   Dono biru desu ka.
f   Tanaka-san no kaisha wa doko desu ka.
g   Sō desu ka. Tanaka-san no uchi wa doko desu ka.

now you're talking!

1 **1•86** Before leaving your hotel to do some sightseeing, you stop to ask the doorman for directions.

- ◆ Greet the doorman (it's morning) and ask where the post office is.
- ● **Ano depāto no tonari desu.**
- ◆ Ask him to repeat what he said.
- ● **Hai, depāto no tonari desu.**
- ◆ Thank him.

2 **1•87** After the post office, you want to go to Hibiya Park. You think you know where it is, but ask a passer-by just to confirm.

- ◆ Attract the passer-by's attention.
- ● **Hai.**
- ◆ Ask if Hibiya Park is over in that direction (pointing).
- ● **Iie, chigaimasu.** (pointing in a different direction) **Asoko desu. Ano hoteru no ushiro desu.**
- ◆ Ask him to speak more slowly.
- ● **Asoko desu. Ano hoteru no ushiro desu.**
- ◆ Say *Oh really?* and thank him.

3 **1•88** In the park, you begin talking to someone who is eating sandwiches on her lunch break.

- ◆ Ask her where she works.
- ● **Ginkō desu.**
- ◆ Ask if the bank is close by.
- ● **Hai, ano biru desu.**
- ◆ Ask where she lives.
- ● **Kamakura desu.**
- ◆ Ask where Kamakura is – is it near Tokyo?
- ● **Hai, sō desu.**

quiz

1 Does **soko** mean *here*, *there* or *over there*?

2 Which one of these is not a building? **ginkō**, **hoteru**, **kōen**, **yūbinkyoku**.

3 How would you tell someone you don't understand?

4 Which famous Japanese department store is mentioned in this unit?

5 When would you ask someone to speak **motto yukkuri, onegai shimasu**?

6 Is **chigaimasu** similar in meaning to **sō desu** or **sō ja arimasen**?

7 What is the difference between **kono biru** and **sono biru**?

8 How would you ask someone to repeat what they've just said?

9 Who would you talk to in a **kōban**?

10 If someone responds to your question with **chigaimasu** are they saying you're right or wrong?

Now check whether you can ...

- ask and say where something is
- ask if it is nearby
- say if a place is here, there or further away from you
- ask someone to repeat something or say it more slowly
- say where you live and work

Don't worry too much about making mistakes. You'll learn much more quickly if you try to express yourself, even if you make a few mistakes, than if you say nothing until you are word perfect. If you need to play for time, you can use phrases like **anō ...** or **ēto ...** (both the equivalent of *umm ...*), **ja** *well* and **Sō desu ne ...** *Let me see ...* Listen out for these phrases in future units.

Mainichi aite imasu

finding out about facilities

asking where someone is

understanding how to find a place

... and asking when it's open

Nihon de wa ...

you can get information about what's going on in town from a number
of sources. At the main Tourist Information Centres (**kankō annaijo**) in
Tokyo, and Kyoto and Narita Airport, there are English-speaking staff
and free maps and tourist newspapers giving information on festivals,
tours and other local events. There are also monthly English-language
magazines published in most of the major cities giving listings for
movies, theatres, concerts, etc., on sale in large bookshops and most of
the major hotels.

Finding out about facilities

1 **2•01** Listen to these key phrases.

Kono chikaku ni ...	Near here ...
... ginkō wa arimasu ka.	... is there a bank?
Hai, pūru ga arimasu.	Yes, there's a pool.
Dorai kuriiningu wa arimasen.	There isn't a dry cleaner's.

2 Can you guess what these words for hotel facilities mean? Many are very similar to the English equivalent.

furonto	bā
toire	raunji
robii	erebētā
pūru	
dorai kuriiningu	

Nihongo de wa ...

the phrase **... ga arimasu** means *There is/are ...* and is used to talk about the existence of something. The word **ga** points out the subject, the thing you're talking about, by coming directly after it. In questions and negative answers *No, there isn't/aren't* you might use **wa** instead of **ga**.

Bā ga arimasu.	*There's a bar.*
Kissaten wa arimasu ka.	*Is there a coffee shop?*
Iie, kissaten wa arimasen.	*No, there isn't a coffee shop.* **G6**

---

3 **2•02** Mr Brown stops a passer-by to ask if there's a bank. Is there or isn't there? Note that the word **ni** shows the location (rather like *in*, *at*) by coming immediately after the place word.

4 **2•03** A tour guide has just announced that the group's hotel has changed. Listen to some people asking him questions about the new hotel and tick the facilities on the notepad in Activity 2.

... and asking where someone is

5   **2•04** Listen to these key phrases.

Tanaka-san wa doko ni imasu ka.	Where's Tanaka-san?
Iie, pūru ni imasen.	He's not in the pool.
Hito ga takusan imasu ne.	There are a lot of people, aren't there!
Nan desu ka.	What is it?

6   **2•05** Listen to a tourist in a hotel asking where a mutual friend, Tanaka-san, might be. Where is he?

Nihongo de wa ...

arimasu/arimasen is only used to talk about the existence of objects (buildings, furniture, etc.). To talk about something living (people, animals, birds – but not plants), use **imasu/imasen**.

Ikeda-san wa asoko ni imasu.	*Ikeda-san is over there.*
Ikeda-san no uchi wa asoko ni arimasu.	*Ikeda-san's house is over there.*

G4

---

7   **2•06** Yamada-san is shopping with a friend when she notices a crowd of people watching a **matsuri** *festival*. Complete the conversation with **arimasu** or **imasu**. Then listen to the audio to check your answers.

Yamada-san	**Asoko ni hito ga takusan .... ne.**
Friend	**Sō desu ne. Nani ga .... ka.**
Yamada-san	**A! Kyō wa matsuri ga ....**
Friend	**Sō desu ka. A! Asoko ni tomodachi ga ....**

8   How would you ask:

- if there is a coffee shop nearby?
- if Yamada-san is in the bar?

Understanding how to find a place

1 **2•07** Listen to these key phrases.

Migi/hidari ni arimasu. It's on the right/left.
Massugu itte, migi desu. Go straight ahead and then turn right.

massugu
straight ahead

hidari
left

migi
right

2 **2•08** Some tourists are going to the park to see the **sakura** *cherry blossoms*. Is the park to the left or the right?

3 **2•09** Later they look for a coffee shop. Listen and make a note in English of the directions.

4 You might want to learn to recognise some Japanese signs in order to help you get around. Here are a few useful ones.

iriguchi
entrance

入
口

deguchi
exit

出
口

o-tearai
*washrooms
/toilets*

お
手
洗

onna
woman

女

otoko
man

男

... and asking when it's open

5 **2•10** Listen to these key phrases.

Suiyōbi wa yasumi desu.	It's closed on Wednesday.
Ashita wa doyōbi desu.	Tomorrow is Saturday.
Kyō wa aite imasu.	It's open today.
Mainichi aite imasu.	It's open every day.

Mon	Getsuyōbi	**Fri**	Kinyōbi
Tues	Kayōbi	**Sat**	Doyōbi
Wed	Suiyōbi	**Sun**	Nichiyōbi
Thur	Mokuyōbi		

6 **2•11** Listen to the person in the **kankō annaijo** giving information to various tourists and fill in the gaps below.

   a swimming pool   closed on ....

   b **sakura matsuri**
        cherry blossom festival   from ....

   c Matsuya Department Store   closed on ....

7 **2•12** Now listen to two phone calls and then decide whether the following are true or false.

		true	false
a	Kimura Dry Cleaning is open every day.		
b	The sports centre is closed tomorrow.		
c	Tomorrow is Wednesday.		

put it all together

1   Look at the pictures and answer the following questions.

     a   b   c

    a   Is Tanaka-san waiting at the exit or entrance?
    b   Is Ms Brown using the correct entrance?
    c   Is it the exit or the entrance which is to the left?

2   How would you answer these questions about your town?

    a   **Pūru wa arimasu ka. Mainichi aite imasu ka.**
    b   **Depāto wa arimasu ka. Yasumi wa nanyōbi desu ka.**
    c   **Anata no uchi no chikaku ni, nani ga arimasu ka.**
    d   **Kōen wa takusan arimasu ka.**

3   Can you say in Japanese which days the following places in your town are open and closed?

    a   bank
    b   library (**toshokan**)
    c   post office

1   **2•13** You've just arrived in a small town and you ask a
     passer-by for some information.

   ◆ Say *Excuse me* and ask if there's a Tourist Information
     Centre nearby.
   ● **Hai, arimasu. Massugu itte, hidari desu.**
   ◆ Repeat the directions you were given and thank him.
   ● **Iie.**

2   **2•14** At the Tourist Information Centre, you ask about
     swimming pools.

   ◆ Ask if there's a pool in the area.
   ● **Hai, kono chikaku ni supōtsu sentā ga arimasu.**
     Supōtsu sentā no naka ni pūru ga arimasu.
   ◆ Ask if it's open tomorrow.
   ● **Hai, aite imasu.**
   ◆ Ask what day it's closed.
   ● **Getsuyōbi desu.**
   ◆ Thank her.

3   **2•15** It takes a while to reach your hotel as there are crowds
     of people in the street, so you ask what's happening at the
     reception desk.

   ◆ Comment that there are a lot of people and ask what's
     going on.
   ● **Kyō wa matsuri desu.**
   ◆ Say *Oh really?* and ask if the festival is on tomorrow, too.
   ● **Hai, kyō mo ashita mo arimasu. Yamashita Kōen no**
     naka desu.
   ◆ Ask where Yamashita Park is.
   ● **Hoteru kara migi desu. Sore kara, massugu desu.**
     Migi ni arimasu.
   ◆ Thank her.

quiz

1 Do you know your **migi** from your **hidari**?

2 If someone asks **Doko ni imasu ka**, are they asking the location of a person or a thing?

3 How would you ask if there's a phone?

4 How would you say that today is Friday?

5 What's a **matsuri**?

6 Which of the following is the odd one out?
kayōbi   nanyōbi   suiyōbi   doyōbi

7 If someone asks the whereabouts of the **kankō annaijo**, what are they looking for?

8 Can you name in Japanese one kind of blossom for which Japan is famous?

9 If you were told the Japanese character on the washroom door said **onna** would the room be for women or men?

10 If you're told that today is a department store's **yasumi** can you go shopping there?

Now check whether you can …

- tell someone what there is in a town
- talk about where a person is
- understand straightforward directions
- ask if a place is open or closed
- recognise the names of the days of the week

The more you listen to the audio, the more confident you'll become with what you've learnt. Don't be afraid to move on and don't worry if you can't remember everything – everyone experiences this at times. It takes time and lots of perseverance to learn a language: practice makes perfect!

Ikura desu ka

understanding prices in yen

... and asking for items

coping in the post office

... and the department store

Nihon de wa ...

a department store is well worth a visit, even if you don't enjoy shopping. Aside from the usual floors for clothes, furniture and household goods, most large department stores will also have a huge food area with lots of free samples, a museum, an art gallery, numerous coffee shops, a whole floor with different kinds of restaurant, and a roof garden which may include a children's playground, garden centre and beer garden. Opening hours are generally 10 a.m. to 8 or 9 p.m., with Saturdays and Sundays being the busiest shopping days.

Understanding prices in yen

1   **2•16** Listen to these key phrases.

Ikura desu ka.	How much is it?/How much are they?
Ringo wa ikura desu ka.	How much are the apples?
¥240 (ni-hyaku yon-jū en) desu.	It's/they're 240 yen.

2   **2•17** Counting large numbers in Japanese is not difficult. A hundred is **hyaku**, so can you tick the numbers below as you hear them?

▨ 400   ▨ 550   ▨ 200   ▨ 780   ▨ 120   ▨ 930

Nihongo de wa ...

large numbers are made up of combinations of the numbers 1 to 9 with **hyaku** *100*, **sen** *1000* and **man** *10,000*.

450	**yon-hyaku go-jū**
2450	**ni-sen yon-hyaku go-jū**
32,450	**san-man ni-sen yon-hyaku go-jū**

There are a few combinations where the pronunciation changes.

300 **san-byaku**	*600* **rop-pyaku**	*800* **hap-pyaku**
3000 **san-zen**		*8000* **has-sen**

---

3   **2•18** Listen to four short conversations and circle the correct prices.

ringo	painappuru	meron	tomato

- apples ¥420   ¥200   ¥240   ● pineapples ¥890   ¥980   ¥870
- melon ¥2700   ¥2770   ¥2270
- apple, pineapple, tomato, melon ¥5100   ¥4500   ¥4100

... and asking for items

4 **2•19** Listen to these key phrases.

Sandoitchi wa arimasu ka.	Do you have any sandwiches?
Hamu sando ga gozaimasu.	We have ham sandwiches. (formal)
... wa gozaimasen.	We don't have ... (formal)
Zenbu de ikura desu ka.	How much is it altogether?

5 **2•20** Ikeda-san is going to Nagoya today for a meeting. He buys some things for the journey at a kiosk on the station platform. Tick the items you hear mentioned.

▒ ham sandwich ▒ chocolate (**chokorēto**) ▒ apple juice
▒ cola ▒ cheese sandwich ▒ orange juice ▒ beer
▒ mixed (**mikkusu**) sandwich ▒ newspaper (**shinbun**)

Listen again and now circle the items he actually bought.

Nihongo de wa ...

people who work in shops, restaurants and hotels use very polite forms of language, so it helps if you can recognise these forms. You don't need to use them yourself.

Gozaimasu is the polite form of **arimasu** (*have, there is/are*).
De gozaimasu is the polite form of **desu** (*is/are*).
Japan Times wa gozaimasen. *We don't have the Japan Times.* (an English-language newspaper)
Zenbu de ¥500 de gozaimasu. *That'll be ¥500 altogether.* **G13**

---

6 **2•21** On the train back to Tokyo, Ikeda-san buys some things from the trolley being wheeled up and down the train.

What does he buy to drink? Can you guess what **poteto chippu** means? How much change (**o-tsuri**) is he given?

Coping in the post office

1 **2•22** Listen to these key phrases.

Igirisu made ikura desu ka.	How much is it to England?
Kōkūbin desu ka.	Is it airmail?
Kōkūbin de, onegai shimasu.	By airmail, please.
¥220 kitte	a ¥220 stamp
¥220 kitte o san-mai kudasai.	Three ¥220 stamps, please.

2 **2•23** Yamada-san is waiting in line at the post office and hears a tourist asking about some **tegami** *letters* she wants to send.

a Where is she sending them?
b How much does it cost for one letter?
c How many letters does she want to send?

Nihongo de wa ...

flat objects such as stamps, postcards, letters, tickets and CDs are counted with **-mai**.

Hagaki o yon-mai kudasai.	*Four postcards, please.*
Nan-mai desu ka.	*How many (would you like)?*

G11

---

3 **2•24** Now it's Yamada-san's turn. She has various things to buy. Listen and fill in the gaps.

Yamada-san	**Kono tegami wa Amerika .... ikura desu ka.**
Assistant	**.................. desu ka.**
Yamada-san	**Hai, sō desu.**
Assistant	**.................. desu.**
Yamada-san	**Sore kara, ¥100 kitte o .... kudasai.**
Assistant	**Hai, dōzo. .... ¥720 en desu.**

... and the department store.

4 **2•25** Listen to these key phrases.

Sore o misete kudasai.	Please could I see that?
Chotto ōkii desu.	It's rather large.
Motto chiisai no wa arimasu ka.	Do you have a smaller one?
Kore, onegai shimasu.	I'll take this.

5 **2•26** Next Yamada-san goes to a department store to buy a birthday present for her father. Listen and tick the key phrases as you hear them. What does she buy and how much is it?

Nihongo de wa ...

to ask for something bigger, cheaper, etc., simply use **motto** *more* before the word – **motto takai** *more expensive*, **motto ōkii** *bigger*. In these sentences, **no** stands for the thing you have been talking about, rather like the English *one/ones*.

Motto yasui kamera wa arimasu ka.	*Do you have any cheaper cameras?*
Motto yasui no wa arimasu ka.	*Do you have any cheaper ones?*
Motto chiisai no o kudasai.	*I'd like a smaller one please.*

---

6 **2•27** Before leaving the store, Yamada-san goes to look at some shoes (**kutsu**). Listen, then say if the following statements are true or false.

		true	false
a	The first pair she tries are too small.		
b	She then tries a size (**saizu**) 23 cm.		
c	She finally buys a pair of shoes.		

7 How would you:

- ask for two ¥120 stamps? • ask if they have a smaller camera?
- say these French shoes are rather expensive?

put it all together

1   Match the English words and phrases with the Japanese.

a	zenbu de	by airmail
b	chotto chiisai	a cheaper one
c	kōkūbin de	altogether
d	o-tsuri	do you have?
e	ikura?	a little small
f	motto yasui no wa	how much?
g	arimasu ka	change

2   Here is your shopping list. How would you ask for these items?

> two ¥85 stamps
> three postcards
> two apples
> apple juice
> crisps

3   A customer is in a department store, buying a belt (**beruto**) as a present. Can you put the lines of dialogue in order?

Customer	Ii desu ne. Ja, kono Itaria no beruto o kudasai.
Customer	Ikura desu ka.
Customer	Nana-sen rop-pyaku en? Chotto takai desu ne. Motto yasui no wa arimasu ka.
Customer	Sumimasen, sono beruto o misete kudasai.
Assistant	Hai. Kono beruto wa ¥3700 desu. Itaria no beruto desu.
Assistant	¥7600 en desu.
Assistant	Kono Furansu no beruto desu ka. Hai, dōzo.

4   If you buy three items each costing the following, and pay for them all with a ¥10,000 note, how much change should you expect?

- go-hyaku san-jū en
- ni-sen yon-hyaku en
- ni-hyaku go-jū en

1   **2•28** You're in the post office, wanting to post a few letters home.

- ◆ Ask how much it is to send this letter to Britain.
- ● **Kōkūbin desu ka.**
- ◆ Say yes, you'd like to send it by airmail.
- ● **¥140 desu.**
- ◆ You have three such letters, so ask for three ¥140 stamps.
- ● **Dōzo. ¥420 desu.**
- ◆ Thank him.

2   **2•29** Next you go to a department store to buy some souvenirs. You see some watches (**tokei**) you like.

- ● **Irasshaimase.**
- ◆ Ask to see that watch over there.
- ● **Hai, dōzo.**
- ◆ When you try it on, you decide it's a bit too small. Ask if there's a bigger one.
- ● **Hai, gozaimasu.**
- ◆ Say it's nice. But you can't see a price tag – ask how much it is.
- ● **¥8500 de gozaimasu.**
- ◆ Say you'd like to take it.

3   **2•30** On the train to Nagoya, you buy some things from the trolley which comes along the corridor.

- ◆ You ask for some apple juice and a cheese sandwich.
- ● **Hai, dōzo.**
- ◆ You notice she has some newspapers on the trolley. Ask if she has the Japan Times.
- ● **Sumimasen. Japan Times wa gozaimasen.**
- ◆ Ask how much it is altogether.
- ● **¥730 de gozaimasu.**
- ◆ You give her a thousand yen.
- ● **Hai, ¥270 no o-tsuri de gozaimasu.**

quiz

1 If you want to buy three postcards, would you use **san-mai** or **mittsu**?
2 If a sales clerk says **gozaimasen** when you ask for something, what does it mean?
3 How much is **ichi-man en**?
4 Would you buy a **shinbun** to eat or to read?
5 Where would you go to buy some **kitte**?
6 Can you go shopping in Japan on Sundays?
7 How would you ask to see *that camera*?
8 How would you ask for something to be sent airmail?
9 Does **motto chiisai** means *bigger* or *smaller*?

Now check whether you can ...

- ask how much something costs
- understand large numbers
- ask for stamps for a particular country
- give some detail about the kind of item you want

As you've seen, there are different ways of counting objects in Japanese, depending on their shape. This isn't as complicated as it sounds – try practising with the following:

-hon   long, slender objects (bottles, pencils, cans of juice)
       biiru ni-hon = *two bottles of beer*
-nin   people
       tomodachi san-nin = *three friends*

However, if you can't remember the appropriate counters, you can always use the **hitotsu**, **futatsu**, **mittsu** system (see Unit 4).

Chekkupointo 2

1 **2•31** Listen to three people at the **kōban** being given directions.
   Follow their route on the map and write down where they're going and
   the letter which corresponds to it on the map.

   a ....

   b ....

   c ....

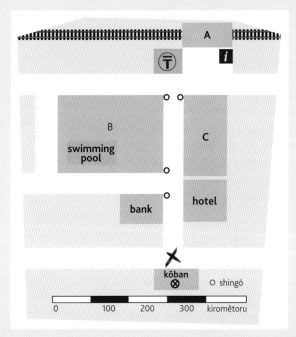

2 Look at the map again and decide which word fits in the gap in
   each sentence.

   | eki   naka   mae   ginkō |

   a **Kōen no** .... **ni pūru ga arimasu.**

   b .... **wa hoteru no mukai ni arimasu.**

   c **Yūbinkyoku wa** .... **no tonari ni arimasu.**

   d **Kankō annaijo wa eki no** .... **ni arimasu.**

3　**2•32** Listen and check whether the prices you hear are the same as the ones on the list. Tick the ones that are correct and change the ones which are wrong.

tomato	¥370
ringo	¥540
banana	¥280
painappuru	¥960
meron	¥1980
miruku	¥130
poteto chippu	¥160
	¥4420

4　**2•33** Listen to someone in a hotel asking at the front desk for some information and then decide whether the statements which follow are true or false.

		true	false
a	Hoteru ni pūru ga arimasu.	☐	☐
b	Hoteru no pūru wa kyō aite imasu.	☐	☐
c	Yūbinkyoku wa hoteru no naka ni arimasu.	☐	☐
d	Yūbinkyoku wa kyō yasumi desu.	☐	☐

5　Find the odd one out.

a	tonari	ushiro	kono	mae	chikaku
b	toire	biru	bā	pūru	raunji
c	motto	doko	ikura	nanyōbi	nani
d	hyaku	sen	man	en	
e	yasui	migi	chiisai	takai	ōkii

6 Which one would you use …

- **a** … when what someone says is incorrect?
- **b** … when you don't understand something?
- **c** … when someone is speaking too quickly?
- **d** … when you think something is rather small?
- **e** … when you want someone to repeat what they said?
- **f** … when you want to be shown something in a shop?

7 Can you fit the days of the week into this grid? Which day of the week fits into the tinted box?

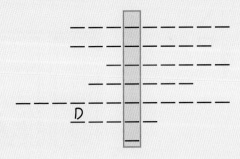

8 Match each sentence to the place in which you're most likely to hear it.

> izakaya   depāto   yūbinkyoku
> kōban   hoteru   eki no kiosuku

a Hyakuni-jū en kitte o yon-mai kudasai.
b Konokutsu wa chotto chiisai desu.
c Biiru o ni-hon kudasai.
d Sumimasen. Guriin Hoteru wa doko desu ka.
e Kono shinbun wa ikura desu ka.
f Bā wa raunji no tonari ni arimasu.

9 Look at these pictures and match the correct Japanese character to the doors.

a   b

c   d

10 Practise answering aloud the following questions about yourself.

O-namae wa?   Uchi wa eki no chikaku desu ka.
O-kuni wa dochira desu ka.   O-tsutome wa dochira desu ka.
O-sumai wa dochira desu ka.

Yoyaku o onegai shimasu

finding a hotel room

booking ahead by phone

checking in at reception

... and asking about facilities

Nihon de wa ...

there is a wide choice of accommodation, ranging from large Western hotels and smaller, modestly priced business hotels to the Japanese-style inns, or **ryokan**.

Rooms in **ryokan** have **tatami** *straw mat* flooring. Outdoor shoes are never worn inside **tatami** rooms and should be left in the lobby. Breakfast and dinner are included in the price and usually served in the rooms at a low table while guests sit on cushions on the floor. At night the **futon**, or *bedding*, is laid out on the **tatami**. Guests can relax in the large communal **furo** *bath* – one for women and one for men.

Finding a hotel room

1   **2•34** Listen to these key phrases.

Konban heya wa arimasu ka.   Do you have a room for tonight?

Shinguru o onegai shimasu.

Daburu o onegai shimasu.

Tsuin o onegai shimasu.

Ip-paku ikura desu ka.   How much is it for one night?
Nan-paku de gozaimasu ka.   For how many nights?

2   **2•35** Listen to Takeda-san at the reception desk of the Yamanaka Hotel wanting to book a room. Tick off the key phrases as you hear them. What kind of room (**heya**) does he want?

Nihongo de wa ...

to ask an 'either/or' question, simply ask two separate questions.
Shinguru desu ka. Tsuin desu ka.
Would you like a single or a double room?
Ip-paku desu ka. Ni-haku desu ka.
Is it for one or two nights?

The number of nights spent in a hotel is counted with **-haku** (in some cases this changes to **paku**):
ip-paku *one night*, **ni-haku, san-paku, yon-haku, go-haku**   **G9**

---

3   **2•36** Now listen to Yamaguchi-san asking about rooms at the Yamanaka Hotel.

   a   How long does she want to stay?
   b   How much is the hotel per night?
   c   What kind of room does she book?

Booking ahead by phone

1   **2•37** Listen to these key phrases.

Moshi moshi.	Hello? (on the phone)
Yoyaku o onegai shimasu.	I'd like to make a reservation.
Itsu deshō ka.	When is it for?
3-gatsu 23-nichi ni heya wa arimasu ka.	Do you have a room on March 23rd?

2   **2•38** Fujimura-san is trying to reserve a room at a busy hotel. When does she want a room and is she successful?

Moshi moshi.

Nihongo de wa ...

the months are said as the number of the month plus **-gatsu**: **ichi-gatsu** *January*, **roku-gatsu** *June*. The alternative ways of saying the numbers 4 (**shi**) and 7 (**shichi**) are used with the months: **shi-gatsu** *April* and **shichi-gatsu** *July*.

The dates are as follows:

1st	**tsuitachi**	*6th*	**muika**	*14th*	**jū-yokka**
2nd	**futsuka**	*7th*	**nanoka**	*20th*	**hatsuka**
3rd	**mikka**	*8th*	**yōka**	*24th*	**ni-jū-yokka**
4th	**yokka**	*9th*	**kokonoka**		
5th	**itsuka**	*10th*	**tōka**		

All the other dates are formed with the number plus **-nichi**: **jū-go-nichi** *15th*, **san-jū-nichi** *30th*

---

3   **2•39** A receptionist is taking two bookings over the phone. Can you work out the dates and type of room they reserve?

	date/s	type of room	
Ikeda-san	....	....	
Wada-san	....	....	

Checking in at reception

1   **2•40** Listen to these key phrases.

Yoyaku shimashita.	I've made a reservation.
O-namae to go-jūsho	Your name and address, please.
o onegai shimasu.	
O-heya wa go-kai de	Your room is on the fifth floor.
gozaimasu.	
Dōzo, kochira e.	Please come this way.

2   **2•41** Fujimura-san is on a business trip. Has she booked a Japanese-style room (**washitsu**) or a Western-style room (**yōshitsu**)?

Nihongo de wa ...

the floors of a building are counted with **-kai: ik-kai, ni-kai, san-gai, yon-kai** etc. The ground floor is counted as **ik-kai**.
Bā wa ik-kai ni arimasu.   *The bar is on the ground floor.*

---

3   **2•42** Listen to this conversation between a receptionist in a large hotel and a guest. Note which floor the various rooms are on.

resutoran	....	**furo**	....
washitsu	....	**bā**	....

4   **2•43** Listen as Yamada-san arrives at a hotel and note whether the following statements are true or false.

		true	false
a	Yamada-san already has a reservation.	▨	▨
b	She fills out a form with her name, address and phone number.	▨	▨
c	She has a Western-style room.	▨	▨
d	Her room is on the second floor.	▨	▨

... and asking about facilities

5   **2•44** Listen to these key phrases.

Shokuji tsuki desu ka.	How about meals?
Ni-shoku tsuki desu.	Two meals are included.
Chōshoku to yūshoku desu.	Breakfast and dinner.
Kono hoteru ni fakkusu wa arimasu ka.	Is there a fax in the hotel?

6   **2•45** One of the guests in a small business hotel is asking about the various facilities and services. Put a tick by the facilities available. Listen out for **sore kara** *and also*.

shokuji   **terebi**   **fakkusu**   **furo**   **shawā**

Nihongo de wa ...

instead of using **furo tsuki desu ka** you can ask about facilities simply by saying the word followed by **wa** and with your voice rising at the end, so the question is implied.

Furo wa?	*How about a bath?*
Shawā wa?	*How about a shower?*

G9

---

7   How would you ask:

- if two meals are included in the price?
- if your room has a shower?
- if the hotel has Western-style and Japanese-style rooms?

put it all together

1 Match the Japanese phrases with the English.

a	**Shokuji tsuki desu ka.**	How about breakfast?
b	**Moshi moshi.**	Is it a Japanese-style room?
c	**Nan-paku desu ka.**	When for?
d	**Chōshoku wa?**	It's on the fourth floor.
e	**Washitsu desu ka.**	Hello?
f	**Yon-kai ni arimasu.**	How many nights?
g	**Itsu deshō ka.**	Are meals included?

2 Complete the following sentences using the pictures below.

a .... o onegai shimasu.
b .... tsuki desu ka.
c .... ni heya wa
   arimasu ka.
d .... tsuki desu ka.

a   b
c   d

3 Recreate the phone conversation by putting the sentences in the correct order.

Guest **18-nichi desu.**
Guest **Ja, onegai shimasu.**
Guest **Shinguru o onegai shimasu. Ip-paku ikura desu ka.**
Guest **Moshi moshi. Yoyaku o onegai shimasu.**

Receptionist **Hai, yoyaku desu ne. Itsu deshō ka.**
Receptionist **Kinyōbi desu ne. Shinguru desu ka. Tsuin desu ka.**
Receptionist **Ip-paku ¥9800 desu.**

4 Can you give the following dates in Japanese?

- today
- Christmas
- your birthday
- New Year's Day

now you're talking!

1 **2•46** Imagine you have just arrived at the Park Hotel and want to book a room.

- **Irasshaimase.**
- ◆ Ask if they have a room for tonight.
- **Shinguru desu ka. Daburu desu ka.**
- ◆ Say you want a single room.
- **Hai, nan-paku desu ka.**
- ◆ Say you'll be staying one night.
- **Hai, gozaimasu.**
- ◆ Ask how much it is for one night.
- **¥12,000 de gozaimasu.**
- ◆ Say you'll take it.

2 **2•47** Now take the part of John Graham, who is having problems with his hotel booking.

- **Irasshaimase.**
- ◆ Say you have a reservation and give your name.
- **Graham-san desu ne. Hai, daburu desu ne.**
- ◆ Say no, that's not correct, it's a single room.
- **Sō desu ka. Shitsurei shimashita. Shinguru, san-paku desu ne.**

- ◆ Say no, it's for two nights.
- **Shitsurei shimashita, o-namae o mō ichido onegai shimasu.**
- ◆ Give your name again.
- **A, John Graham-san desu ne. Dōmo shitsurei shimashita. Shinguru, ni-haku no yoyaku desu ne.**
- ◆ Say yes, that's right.

quiz

1 When would you say **moshi moshi**?
2 If you were quoted a hotel price which was **chōshoku tsuki**, would you expect breakfast to be included?
3 Where would you find **tatami** and **futon**?
4 When is **shi-gatsu tsuitachi**?
5 If someone asked you **nan-paku**, what information would you give them?
6 Which would you expect to find in a **ryokan – washitsu** or **yōshitsu**?
7 What would you do with a **furo**?
8 How would you say the 20th of the month?

Now check whether you can ...

● say you have a reservation
● ask for a room in a hotel and specify double or single, Japanese-style or Western-style
● ask if meals are included
● say how long you want the room for and specify dates
● ask if the room has a bath, shower or other facilities

Don't worry too much if you can't always remember the appropriate way of counting just at the moment you need it. If, for example, you remember that the counter for days of the month is **nichi** but can't remember the exceptions, then use **-nichi**. If you say **ni-nichi** instead of the correct **futsuka**, it may not be correct, but people will still understand you. Some of the counters have slight variations – **kai** changes to **gai** after **san**. There is no obvious pattern to learn, but don't worry, you will get used to them as you hear them.

Yokohama made ichi-mai

finding out train times

buying tickets

asking about public transport

taking a taxi

Nihon de wa ...

the **shinkansen** *bullet trains* are high-speed trains that link major cities. The local train (**densha**) networks are excellent: safe and always reliable. In larger cities, you'll find some station signs in English. However, on the buses (**basu**), you'll have to ask if the bus is going your way, as destinations are only written in Japanese characters on the front of the bus.

You can flag down a taxi (**takushii**) anywhere. It's helpful to have the address of your destination written down in Japanese. All taxis have meters so you can see how much you'll need to pay. And one more great advantage – there's no tipping.

Finding out train times

1 2•48 Listen to these key phrases.

Tsugi no Nagoya yuki wa nan-ji desu ka.	What time is the next (train) for Nagoya?
Nagoya yuki	bound for Nagoya
Nan-ji ni tsukimasu ka.	At what time does it arrive?
jū-ji han ni	at 10.30
hachi-ji han ni	at 8.30

Nihongo de wa …

to say the time, add **-ji** to the number (for 4 and 7, use **yo** and **shichi**) – 2 o'clock **ni-ji**, 4 o'clock **yo-ji**, 12 o'clock **jū-ni-ji**. To give the half hour, add **han** *half* – 3.30 **san-ji han**, 8.30 **hachi-ji han**.
Ku-ji han ni tsukimasu. *It arrives at 9.30.*

---

2 2•49 Listen to someone asking for train times and fill in the gaps below.

Tourist	**Sumimasen. .... Nagoya yuki wa nan-ji desu ka.**
Assistant	**................................ desu.**
Tourist	**................................ desu ka. Hai. Sore kara, Nagoya wa .... tsukimasu ka.**
Assistant	**Nagoya wa .... ni tsukimasu.**
Tourist	**................................ desu ne. Arigatō.**

3 2•50 Listen to some people asking about the times of various trains, then fill in the table below.

Destination	Departure time	Arrival time
Ōsaka		
Kyōto		

... and buying tickets

4 **2•51** Listen to these key phrases.

Tōkyō made ikura desu ka.	How much is it to Tokyo?
Katamichi desu ka. Ōfuku desu ka.	Single or return?
Yokohama made ichi-mai.	One to Yokohama.
Shitei-seki desu ka. Jiyū-seki desu ka.	Reserved seat or unreserved seat?
jū-ichi-ji san-jū-go-fun hatsu	11.35 departure

5 **2•52** Listen as two tourists ask for help to use the ticket machines (**jidō hanbaiki**) at the station. Choose the correct answers.

	No of tickets	Type	Price
Tōkyō	1 / 2 / 3	single / return	¥30,300 / ¥3,300 / ¥13,100
Yokohama	1 / 2 / 3	single / return	¥14,800 / ¥41,000 / ¥4,800

Nihongo de wa ...

for minutes after the hour, add **-fun** or **-pun: ip-pun** *one minute*: **ni-fun, san-pun, yon-pun, go-fun, rop-pun, nana-fun, hap-pun, kyū-fun, jup-pun.**
Hachi-ji jup-pun hatsu no densha. *The train that leaves at 8.10.*
Ichi-ji yon-jū-go-fun hatsu no basu. *The bus that leaves at 1.45.*

---

6 **2•53** Listen to someone buying a ticket for the **shinkansen**. Then say if the following statements are true or false.

		true	false
a	The woman wants to travel on March 9th.		
b	She buys tickets for the 11.45 train to Kobe.		
c	She wants reserved seats.		
d	She buys two singles.		
e	The tickets cost ¥16,600.		
f	The train arrives in Kobe at 13.15.		

Asking about public transport

1 **2•54** Listen to these key phrases.

Kono densha wa Yokohama e ikimasu ka.	Does this train go to Yokohama?
Hai, ikimasu.	Yes, it does.
Iie, ikimasen.	No, it doesn't.
Nan-ban sen desu ka.	Which platform number?
Ni-ban sen desu.	Platform number 2.

2 **2•55** Listen to Mr Brown trying to find his way around the Tokyo train system. Where does he want to go and does the train go there? Note that **e** *to, towards* comes after the name of the place.

Nihongo de wa ...

verbs come at the end of a sentence, except when followed by **ka**.

Tōkyō e ikimasu.	*I'm going to Tokyo.*
Kono basu wa Shibuya e ikimasu ka.	*Is this bus going to Shibuya?*

G5

To form a negative, change the **-masu** ending to **-masen**.

Kono densha wa Ginza e ikimasen.	*This train doesn't go to Ginza.*
San-ji ni tsukimasen.	*It doesn't arrive at 3 o'clock.*

G2

---

3 **2•56** Now listen to two more tourists finding their way around and fill in the information below.

a Train: to .... platform ....

b ....: to Shibuya no. ....

Taking a taxi

1   **2•57** Listen to these key phrases.

Sumitomo Biru made onegai shimasu.	To the Sumitomo Building, please.
Koko de ii desu.	This is fine here.
Wakarimashita.	I see./I understand.
Ryōshūsho o onegai shimasu.	Could I have a receipt, please?

2   **2•58** Ogawa-san takes a taxi to a business appointment. Tick the key phrases as you hear them. How much does the taxi cost?

¥ ....

3   **2•59** The taxi driver finds it hard to understand where his next passenger wants to go. What does the passenger point out on the hotel card (**kādo**)?

4   **2•59** Listen again and choose the correct answer below.

   a   The man wants to go to the   Green Hotel/Hilton Hotel.
   b   The hotel is in   Shinjuku/Ginza.

Nihon de wa ...

don't stand too close to the taxi as it pulls up – the door will swing open for you as the driver opens it automatically. He'll also close it again after you've got in, and he'll open it again at your destination after you've paid your fare.

---

5   How would you ask:

- if this train is going to Kobe?
- which platform the Osaka train leaves from?
- the taxi driver to take you to Tokyo station?

put it all together

1 Select the answer for each question.

a	Nan-ji ni tsukimasu ka.	1	Iie, ikimasen.
b	Katamichi desu ka.	2	13.30 desu.
c	Nagoya made ikura desu ka.	3	Iie, shitei-seki desu.
d	Kōbe-yuki wa nan-ban sen desu ka.	4	Iie, ōfuku desu.
e	Kono basu wa Tōkyō e ikimasu ka.	5	¥2450 desu.
f	Jiyū-seki desu ka.	6	San-ban sen desu.

2 Work out how you would say the following times in Japanese:

3 Where would you be if you were saying:

    a Hiruton Hoteru made onegai shimasu.
    b Kono densha wa Kōbe e ikimasu ka.
    c Nagoya yuki, ni-mai kudasai.
    d Kono basu wa Shibuya yuki desu ka.

4 Complete these sentences with **wa**, **ni** or **e**.

    a Kono densha wa nan-ji .... tsukimasu ka.
    b Sumimasen. Dono basu wa Ginza .... ikimasu ka.
    c Watashi wa ashita Hiroshima.............. ikimasu.
    d Tsugi no Nagoya yuki .... nan-ji desu ka.
    e Hachi-ji .... tsukimasu.
    f Ano basu .... Shibuya yuki desu ka.

now you're talking!

1 **2•60** Imagine you want to go to Hiroshima on the
shinkansen and you'd like some help with the ticket
machine.

- ◆ Get the attention of the person behind you in the queue
  and ask how much it is to Hiroshima.
- ● **Hiroshima desu ne. Katamichi desu ka.**
- ◆ Say no, you want a return.
- ● **Hai. Nan-mai desu ka.**
- ◆ You just want one ticket.
- ● **Hai, Hiroshima yuki, katamichi, ichi-mai desu ne.**
  ¥14,350 desu.
- ◆ Repeat what he said in order to confirm the amount. Then
  say thank you.

2 **2•61** Now you need to find the right train. Ask at the ticket
barrier.

- ◆ Ask the time of the next train to Hiroshima.
- ● **Hai, 9.25 desu.**
- ◆ Confirm the time, then ask what time it arrives in
  Hiroshima.
- ● **13.05 ni tsukimasu.**
- ◆ Now ask which platform.
- ● **Hachi-ban sen desu.**
- ◆ Thank her.

quiz

1 If you take the **shinkansen** to Yokohama, are you travelling by train or bus?

2 What sort of ticket is a **jiyū-seki**?

3 If you hear a station announcement including the phrase **hachi-ji hatsu**, is it about a departure or an arrival?

4 Would you buy a **katamichi** ticket if you want to return later today?

5 Who would you be speaking to if you said **Koko de ii desu**?

6 What would you be given if you asked for a **ryōshūsho**?

7 How would you say you understand something?

8 Where would you go if you were told your train was leaving from **hachi-ban sen**?

Now check whether you can ...

- ask what time trains (or other means of transport) depart and arrive
- find out what platform a train leaves from
- ask for a single or return ticket
- ask for a reserved or unreserved seat
- tell a taxi driver where you want to go
- ask for a receipt
- say you've understood

> When learning a language, it can be easy to underestimate how much you know. Go back occasionally to one of the early units to prove to yourself how much you've learnt. Think also about what you find easy ... and difficult. If you can identify your strengths and weaknesses, you can build on your strengths and find ways of compensating for the weaknesses.

Itadakimasu!

saying what you like and don't like

asking about items on the menu

ordering a meal

paying compliments

Nihon de wa ...

there is an enormous variety of places to eat; from noodle bars and street stalls, a good source of **bentō** *boxed lunch*, to hugely expensive restaurants. For a modestly-priced meal try the **setto** *set menu*; **mōningu setto** *set breakfast menu* or **ranchi setto** *set lunch menu*. Menus are written in Japanese, but choosing an appropriate restaurant is not difficult as many have a display case with astonishingly realistic wax models of the food for sale, all priced. So if you don't know the name of something, you can always bring the waiter to the display window and point. Itadakimasu!

Saying what you like and don't like

1 **2•62** Listen to these key phrases.

Itaria ryōri wa dō desu ka.	How about Italian food?
Piza ga suki desu.	I like pizza.
Amari suki ja arimasen.	I don't really like it. (with negative)
Karē ga kirai desu.	I dislike curry.

2 **2•63** Listen to Takahashi-san and Ikeda-san discussing where to go to eat and tick the key phrases as you hear them. Do they decide to have **piza** *pizza*, **karē** *curry* or **sushi** (bite-sized delicacies served on vinegared rice)?

Nihongo de wa ...

ga is used when stating what you like or dislike. In questions and negative sentences, **wa** is often used.

Sakana ga dai suki desu.	*I love fish.*
... ga suki desu.	*I like fish.*
... wa suki ja arimasen.	*I don't like fish.*
... wa kirai ja arimasen.	*I don't dislike fish./It's OK.*
... ga dai kirai desu.	*I hate fish.*
... ga kirai desu.	*I dislike fish.* **G6**

3 **2•64** Listen to Yamada-san talking to an American friend about some typical Japanese foods and drinks and number them 1 to 5 in order from her favourite to that which she most dislikes.

sashimi
soba *noodles*
sushi
tōfu
yakitori (barbecued pieces
of chicken)

Asking about items on the menu

1 **2•65** Listen to these key phrases.

Nan-mei sama desu ka.	For how many people? (formal)
Roku-nin desu.	Six people.
... wa Eigo de nan desu ka.	What is ... in English?

2 **2•66** A waiter shows two groups of people to their tables in a restaurant. How many people are there in each group?

1st group .... 2nd group ....

Nihongo de wa ...

use the suffix **-nin** to talk about numbers of people. Exceptions are **hitori** *one person* and **futari** *two people*.

tomodachi san-nin	*three friends*
Nihon-jin hitori to Igirisu-jin futari	*one Japanese person and two British people*

G11

---

3 **2•67** One of the customers is English. Listen as she asks her friend about various Japanese items that are pictured on the menu. Match the items with the English descriptions, then tick the item she decides to order.

yakizakana   **sashimi**   **sakana**

niku   **tonkatsu**   **yakiniku**

a fish
b grilled meat
c grilled fish
d raw fish
e meat
f pork cutlet

4 How would you:

- ask what **sashimi** is in English?
- say you really like Japanese food?
- say you don't like raw fish very much?

Ordering a meal

1 **2•68** Listen to these key phrases.

O-kimari desu ka.	Have you decided?
Raisu ni nasaimasu ka. Pan ni nasaimasu ka.	Would you like rice or bread?
O-nomimono wa?	And to drink?
Biiru o ip-pon.	One bottle of beer.
Shōshō o-machi kudasai.	One moment, please.

2 **2•69** Listen to two people in a fast-food restaurant deciding which **ranchi setto** to have and write what they order below.

Man ....

Woman ....

> hanbāgā setto
> sushi setto
> yakizakana setto
> pan
> raisu
> biiru
> kōra

Nihongo de wa ...

long, thin objects (bottles of beer, pens, sticks of barbecued **yakitori**) are counted with the suffix **-hon** (in some cases, this changes to **-pon** or **-bon**): **ip-pon, ni-hon, san-bon, yon-hon, go-hon, rop-pon, nana-hon, hap-pon, kyū-hon, jup-pon.**

Biiru o mō ip-pon kudasai.	*Another (bottle of) beer, please.*
Yakitori o yon-hon kudasai.	*Four yakitori, please.*
Nan-bon desu ka.	*How many?* **G11**

3 **2•70** Listen to Ikeda-san and a colleague having a drink after work in a small **yakitori-ya** *yakitori shop* and fill in the gaps below.

Owner	Irasshaimase. O-kimari desu ka.
Ikeda-san	Hai, yakitori o ....
Owner	Yakitori desu ne.
	Hai. .... desu ka.
Ikeda-san	.... kudasai.
Owner	.... wa?
Ikeda-san	Biiru o .... kudasai.

... and paying compliments

4   **2•71** Listen to these key phrases.

Ii nioi desu ne!	Smells good, doesn't it!
Oishi-sō desu ne!	It looks delicious, doesn't it!
Dō desu ka.	How is it?
Dō deshita ka.	How was it?
Totemo oishikatta desu.	It was really delicious.

5   **2•72** Ikeda-san and his friend are sitting at a bar, where they watch the owner grilling some **shiitake** mushrooms on sticks. Tick any of the key phrases which you hear. Does Ikeda-san try the **shiitake**?

Nihongo de wa ...

adjectives have a different form when you are describing something in the past:

is delicious	**oishii**	*was delicious*	**oishikatta**
is hot	**atsui**	*was hot*	**atsukatta**
is expensive	**takai**	*was expensive*	**takakatta**

There is one irregular adjective: **ii** *good*, **yokatta** *was good*.   **G12**

---

6   **2•73** Yamada-san and her friend are in a restaurant. Listen to their conversation, then tick the correct options below.

a	The two friends	have just arrived.		are just leaving.	
b	Yamada-san asks for	the bill.		one more beer.	
c	Yamada-san ate	fish.		meat.	
d	The bill comes to	¥8500.		¥6500.	
e	They think the restaurant is	cheap.		expensive.	

7   How would you say:

- *This* **yakitori** *looks good?*
- *That restaurant was expensive?*

put it all together

1   Match the Japanese phrases with the English.

a	**Oishikatta desu.**	Smells good, doesn't it!
b	**Roku-nin desu.**	How is it?
c	**Suki ja arimasen.**	It was delicious.
d	**Ii nioi desu ne.**	I love it.
e	**O-nomimono wa?**	There are six people.
f	**Dai suki desu.**	I don't like it.
g	**Dō desu ka.**	Anything to drink?

2   How would you say that this person likes, dislikes, or doesn't mind the following?

a fish   b Japanese beer

c sake   d raw fish

e Italian food

 suki desu

 amari suki ja arimasen

kirai desu

3   Rearrange these sentences into the order you would be likely to hear them in a restaurant.

a   **Biiru o ni-hon kudasai.**
b   **O-kimari desu ka.**
c   **Shōshō o-machi kudasai.**
d   **O-nomimono wa?**
e   **Oishikatta desu.**
f   **San-nin desu.**

4   Choose the most appropriate response to these questions.

a   **Yakizakana wa dō deshita ka.**
b   **Sono atarashii resutoran wa dō deshita ka.**
c   **Indo wa dō deshita ka.**

Atsukatta desu.

Oishikatta desu.

Takakatta desu.

now you're talking!

1 **2•74** You are in a restaurant having lunch with some Japanese friends. One of them asks what you're going to have.

- **Nani ni shimasu ka.**
- ◆ Point to a picture on the menu, and ask what this is.
- **Tonkatsu desu.**
- ◆ Ask what **tonkatsu** is in English.
- *Pork cutlet* **desu. Niku wa suki desu ka.**
- ◆ You reply *Not really*.
- **Yakizakana wa dō desu ka.**
- ◆ Say yes, you'll have grilled fish.

2 **2•75** The waiter comes to take your order.

- **O-kimari desu ka.**
- ◆ You've changed your mind, you'll have meat after all. You ask for the hamburger set meal.
- **Hai. Pan ni nasaimasu ka. Raisu ni nasaimasu ka.**
- ◆ Say *Bread, please*.
- **O-nomimono wa?**
- ◆ You'll have a beer.
- **Ip-pon desu ka.**
- ◆ They're only small bottles and your friends want beer too, so order three bottles.
- **Hai, shōshō o-machi kudasai.**

3 **2•76** You've finished your meal and are getting ready to leave. Your friend asks about the meal.

- **Hanbāgā wa dō deshita ka.**
- ◆ Say it is delicious.
- **Ii desu ne.**
- ◆ Get the waiter's attention and ask for the bill.
- **Hai, ¥9450 desu.**
- ◆ Thank him for the meal as you leave.

quiz

1 Is **tonkatsu** fish or meat?

2 If a friend said **sake ga kirai desu**, would you pour some for him?

3 If five of you go to a restaurant, how would you answer when the waiter asks **nan-mei sama desu ka**?

4 How would you say you really like Japanese food?

5 Which is raw fish on balls of rice, **sushi** or **sashimi**?

6 What does the **yaki-** mean in **yakizakana** and **yakiniku**?

7 If someone says **Oishi-sō desu ne** about a dish, have they tasted it yet?

8 What does the waiter want to know if he asks **O-nomimono wa**?

9 If someone says a meal was **takakatta**, how does he feel about it?

Now check whether you can ...

- say what you like and dislike
- ask others what they like
- say how many people there are in your group
- ask about items on the menu
- order food and drink
- pay compliments

Omedetō! *Congratulations!* You have reached the end of **Talk Japanese**.

And now prepare yourself for the final *Checkpoint* with some revision. Listen to the conversations again – the more you listen, the more confident you will become. You can test your knowledge of the key phrases by covering up the English on the lists. Look back at the final pages of each unit and use the quizzes and checklists to assess how much you remember.

Chekkupointo 3

Imagine you've just arrived in Japan on holiday …

1 You've taken the train from the airport into Tokyo and now you need to take a taxi to your hotel, the Shinjuku Ōtani. Which of the following would you say to the taxi driver?

   a **Watashi no hoteru wa Shinjuku Ōtani desu.**
   b **Shinjuku Ōtani Hoteru made onegai shimasu.**
   c **Shinjuku Ōtani Hoteru wa dochira desu ka.**

2 2•77 When you arrive at your hotel, there are some people in front of you enquiring about rooms. Listen to the conversation and say if the sentences below are true or false.

		true	false
a	The man will stay in the hotel tonight.	☐	☐
b	He books a twin room.	☐	☐
c	Today is Wednesday.	☐	☐
d	He's staying for three nights.	☐	☐
e	He'll be leaving on February 25th.	☐	☐

3 2•78 Now it's your turn to check in. Listen to the receptionist and make a note of the three things she asks you to write down, and also which floor your room is on.

   a ....
   b ....
   c ....
   d .... floor.

   Dōzo, kochira e.

4 2•79 You go to a hotel shop to buy some souvenirs. Listen to another customer in the shop.

   a How much was each item?
   b How many did he buy?
   c How much did he spend altogether?

5   Where did you hear these snatches of conversation?
    Match each sentence to the appropriate location.

    a   Ip-paku ikura desu ka.
    b   Kono kutsu wa chotto ōkii desu.
        Motto chiisai no wa arimasu ka.
    c   Tsugi no Yokohama yuki wa nan-ji desu ka.
    d   Hai, massugu itte, migi desu. Seibu depāto
        wa migi ni arimasu.
    e   Sumimasen, biiru o ni-hon kudasai.
    f   ¥230 kitte o yon-mai kudasai.

    > hoteru no bā
    > yūbinkyoku
    > hoteru
    > eki
    > kōban
    > depāto

6   In the evening, you chat to another guest about jobs, homes and
    families. What questions would you ask, if these are his responses?

    a   …………………………………………………
        Enjinia desu.
    b   …………………………………………………
        Iie, Tōkyō ja arimasen. Watashi no apāto wa Yokohama desu.
    c   …………………………………………………
        Kanai wa 32-sai desu.
    d   …………………………………………………
        Kanai no namae wa Tomoko desu.

7   Later in the evening you go out with a Japanese colleague. Rearrange
    the words to form questions you might hear in the restaurant. Then
    match them to the appropriate responses.

    a   ryōri / suki / ka / Itaria / desu / wa
    b   sama / desu / ka / nan-mei
    c   Eigo / yakizakana / wa / ka / nan / desu / de
    d   ni / nasaimasu / ka / nani
    e   dō / yakiniku / ka / deshita / wa

    1   Tonkatsu o kudasai.
    2   Iie, amari suki ja arimasen.
    3   Oishikatta desu.
    4   Go-nin desu.
    5   'Grilled fish' desu.

8 Fill in the gaps to complete the crossword.

Across

1 Kono hoteru ni pūru wa .... ka.

6 Nihon ryōri ga dai .... desu.

7 Kōhii wa .... desu ka.

8 Pan ni nasaimasu ka. .... ni nasaimasu ka.

11 .... chiisai desu. Chotto ōkii no wa arimasu ka.

13 .... desu ka. Katamichi desu ka.

15 Kono densha wa Tōkyō .... desu ka.

18 Yakizakana wa .... oishii desu ne.

19 Kyō wa .... na tenki desu ne.

Down

1 Dōmo ....

2 Tanaka-san wa doko ni .... ka.

3 Indo ryōri wa .... suki ja arimasen.

4 Kōen wa eki no .... ni arimasu.

5 Nan-mei sama desu ka. San-................. desu.

9 Biiru ni-hon................. o-sake ip-pon kudasai.

10 Hai, ... sama de, genki desu.

12 .... no Nagoya yuki wa nan-ji desu ka.

14 Heya wa zenbu o-................. tsuki desu.

16 Sumimasen, ... nan-ji desu ka.

17 Kono resutoran .... yakizakana wa oishii desu.

Written Japanese

The Japanese writing system is made up of three different kinds of characters, **kanji**, **hiragana** and **katakana**. **Kanji** characters originally came from China and each has a specific meaning. **Hiragana** are phonetic characters that are used to write words which have no **kanji** equivalent and for adding on to **kanji** to form different word endings. **Katakana** characters are used to write imported words, such as **kōhii**, **enjinia**, **hoteru** and foreign names like **Furansu** or your own names.

Japanese can be written horizontally or vertically. When written vertically, it begins on the right-hand side of the page and works towards the left.

The chart below shows both **katakana** characters (next to their equivalent sounds in **romaji**) and **hiragana** characters (in brackets).

a ア (あ)	i イ (い)	u ウ (う)	e エ (え)	o オ (お)
ka カ (か)	ki キ (き)	ku ク (く)	ke ケ (け)	ko コ (こ)
ga ガ (が)	gi ギ (ぎ)	gu グ (ぐ)	ge ゲ (げ)	go ゴ (ご)
sa サ (さ)	shi シ (し)	su ス (す)	se セ (せ)	so ソ (そ)
za ザ (ざ)	ji ジ (じ)	zu ズ (ず)	ze ゼ (ぜ)	zo ゾ (ぞ)
ta タ (た)	chi チ (ち)	tsu ツ (つ)	te テ (て)	to ト (と)
da ダ (だ)	ji ヂ (ぢ)	zu ヅ (づ)	de デ (で)	do ド (ど)
na ナ (な)	ni ニ (に)	nu ヌ (ぬ)	ne ネ (ね)	no ノ (の)
ha ハ (は)	hi ヒ (ひ)	fu フ (ふ)	he ヘ (へ)	ho ホ (ほ)
ba バ (ば)	bi ビ (び)	bu ブ (ぶ)	be ベ (べ)	bo ボ (ぼ)
pa パ (ぱ)	pi ピ (ぴ)	pu プ (ぷ)	pe ペ (ぺ)	po ポ (ぽ)
ma マ (ま)	mi ミ (み)	mu ム (む)	me メ (め)	mo モ (も)
ya ヤ (や)		yu ユ (ゆ)		yo ヨ (よ)
ra ラ (ら)	ri リ (り)	ru ル (る)	re レ (れ)	ro ロ (ろ)
wa ワ (わ)				o ヲ (を)

n ン (ん)

An advantage of knowing some **katakana** is that, having worked out what a word says, the chances are good that you'll understand its meaning, as it probably originated from English. Using the chart, see if you can work out how to read the words opposite. You need to know that a line after a **katakana** character makes the vowel sound long (represented in **romaji** with a line over the letter, eg コーラ **kōra**).

1 Look at the menu below. Can you work out what these items are?

コーヒー	¥380
アイスコーヒー	¥420
ココア	¥350
コカコーラ	¥380
ミルク	¥320
アイスクリーム	¥380
トースト	¥380
ケーキ	¥420
カレーライス	¥700
ステーキ	¥1900

2 Look at the atlas index below. Can you work out the names of the countries?

イスラエル	16
イタリア	13
イラク	18
イラン	17

3 Can you work out what these items are? You'll find them in most households.

ステレオ	....
エアコン	....
カメラ	....
トースター	....
アイロン	....
タオル	....

Transcripts and answers

This section contains scripts of all the conversations. Answers which consist of words and phrases from the conversations are given in bold type in the scripts. Other answers are given separately.

Unit 1

Pages 8 & 9 Saying hello and goodbye

2 • Ogawa-san, ohayō.
  ◆ Ohayō gozaimasu.
  • Itō-san, ohayō.
  ◆ A! Yamada-san! Ohayō.
  • Ikeda-san, ohayō gozaimasu.
  ◆ Ohayō.

3 • Tanaka-san? **Konnichiwa.**
  ◆ A, Yamada-san! Konnichiwa.

4 • Komatsu-san, konnichiwa.
  ◆ A, konnichiwa.
  afternoon
  • Kimura-san, ohayō gozaimasu.
  ◆ Yamada-san, ohayō.
  morning
  • Konbanwa, Nishimura-san.
  ◆ Yamada-san? A, konbanwa.
  evening

6 • Ja, **shitsurei shimasu.**
  ◆ A, Yamada-san, **sayōnara.**
  • **Sayōnara.**

7 • Oyasumi nasai.
  ◆ A, **oyasumi nasai.**
  • **Oyasumi.**

8 • Ohayō gozaimasu.
  ◆ Shitsurei shimasu.
  • Konbanwa.
  ◆ Oyasumi nasai.

Pages 10 & 11 Introducing yourself and getting to know people

2 • Ohayō gozaimasu.
  ◆ **Hashimoto Tarō** desu.
  • Hashimoto-san, ohayō gozaimasu.

  ◆ Suzuki desu. **Suzuki Midori.**
  • Suzuki-san, ohayō gozaimasu.
  ◆ Ikeda desu.
  • Ikeda Haruo-san?
  ◆ Hai, **Ikeda Haruo** desu.
  • Ohayō gozaimasu.
  ◆ Ogawa desu. **Ogawa Akiko** desu.
  • Hai, Ogawa-san.
  hai = yes

3 • **Hajimemashite. Watashi wa** Ikeda Haruo **desu.**
  ◆ Hajimemashite. Ogawa Akiko desu. **Dōzo yoroshiku.**
  • Dōzo yoroshiku.

4 • Hajimemashite. Suzuki Midori desu. Dōzo yoroshiku.

6 • Shitsurei desu ga, Nishimura-san desu ka.
  ◆ Iie, **Kimura** desu.
  • A, Kimura-san desu ka.
  ◆ Hai, sō desu.
  iie = no

7 • **Ohayō** gozaimasu.
  ◆ **Ohayō** gozaimasu. **Shitsurei** desu ga, o-namae wa?
  • Hashimoto desu.
  ◆ Hashimoto-**san** desu ka.
  • Hai, **sō** desu.

Page 12 Put it all together

1 a Hai, sō desu; b Dōzo yoroshiku;
  c Hajimemashite; d Oyasumi nasai;
  e Shitsurei shimasu; f Sō desu ka;
  g Konbanwa; h Ohayō gozaimasu;
  i O-namae wa?

2 a Ohayō gozaimasu; b Shitsurei shimasu; c Konnichiwa.

Page 13 Now you're talking!

1 • **Ohayō gozaimasu.**
  ◆ Ohayō gozaimasu. Shitsurei desu ga, o-namae wa?

- **Steve Wilson desu.**
- ◆ Wilson-san desu ka.
- **Hai, sō desu.**

2 ● **Sakai Keiko-san desu ka.**
- ◆ Hai, sō desu. Sakai Keiko-san desu.
- **A, sō desu ka.**

3 ● Hajimemashite. Kimura Akiko.
  Dōzo yoroshiku.
- ◆ **Hajimemashite. Steve Wilson desu. Dōzo yoroshiku.**

4 ● **Kimura-san, shitsurei shimasu.**
- ◆ Shitsurei shimasu.

5 ● **Itō-san, konbanwa.**
- ◆ Konbanwa.
- **Oyasumi nasai.**

Page 14 Quiz

1 from late morning until early evening; *2* no, you would say it in the evening before you go to bed; *3* you would answer with your name; *4* konbanwa; *5* (ohayō) gozaimasu; *6* (watashi wa) Tanaka Keiko desu; *7* goodbye; *8* when introducing yourself to someone; *9* family names; *10* it's a question.

Unit 2

Pages 16 & 17 Talking about your nationality and where you're from

2 ● Shitsurei desu ga …
- ◆ Hai.
- Amerika-jin desu ka.
- ◆ Hai, sō desu. **Amerika-jin** desu.
- Arigatō gozaimasu.
- ◆ Ohayō gozaimasu. Shitsurei desu ga, Amerika-jin desu ka.
- lie, Amerika-jin ja arimasen. Watashi wa **Igirisu-jin** desu.
- ◆ A, sō desu ka. Igirisu-jin desu ka.
- Hai, sō desu.
- ◆ Arigatō.
- Konnichiwa.
- Konnichiwa.

- ● Shitsurei desu ga, Amerika-jin desu ka.
- ◆ lie, watashi wa **Ōsutoraria-jin** desu.
- ● Hai, arigatō gozaimasu.
Visitor 1 is American; visitor 2 is English; visitor 3 is Australian.

3 Nihon **Nihon-jin** *Japanese;* Igirisu **Igirisu-jin** *English;* Amerika **Amerika-jin** *American;* Sukottorando **Sukottorando-jin** *Scottish;* Uēruzu **Uēruzu-jin** *Welsh;* Ōsutoraria **Ōsutoraria-jin** *Australian;* Airurando **Airurando-jin** *Irish;* Kanada **Kanada-jin** *Canadian*

6 ● Shitsurei desu ga, **o-kuni** wa dochira desu ka.
- ◆ **Igirisu** desu.
- ● Sō desu ka. Rondon **desu ka.**
- ◆ lie, Rondon **ja arimasen.** Manchesutā desu.

7 Mr Jones is not from California.

Page 18 Saying what you do for a living

2 ● Ogawa-san, o-shigoto wa?
- ◆ Watashi wa gakusei desu.
- ● Gakusei desu ka.
- ◆ Hai, sō desu.
- ● Hashimoto-san mo gakusei desu ka.
- ◆ lie, watashi wa enjinia desu.
- ● A, sō desu ka. Tōkyō desu ka.
- ◆ Hai, kaisha wa Tōkyō desu.
- ● Kimura-san wa?
- ◆ Watashi wa shufu desu.
Ogawa-san is a student; Hashimoto-san is an engineer; Kimura-san is a housewife.

3 ● Hashimoto-san wa Nihon-jin desu. Kaishain desu. Kaisha wa Ōsaka desu.
- ◆ Green-san wa Igirisu-jin desu. Enjinia desu. Kaisha wa Rondon desu.

Page 19 Giving your phone number

2 • Yamada-san no nai-sen bangō wa?
  ◆ Watashi wa **san yon hachi** desu.
  • Arigatō. Ogawa-san wa?
  ◆ Hai, watashi wa **kyū ni roku** desu.
  • Kyū ni roku. Hai. Tanaka-san wa?
  ◆ **Hachi ichi go** desu
  • Arigatō. Ishii-san wa?
  ◆ Watashi no nai-sen bangō wa **go nana nana** desu.

4 • Hirano-san, shitsurei desu ga, denwa bangō wa?
  ◆ Hai, watashi no denwa bangō wa **zero san no yon hachi yon san no san san ichi ichi** desu.
  • Matsumoto-san, denwa bangō wa nan-ban desu ka.
  ◆ Kaisha no denwa bangō desu ka.
  • Hai, sō desu.
  ◆ **Zero yon nana ni no roku san no kyū yon yon go** desu.
  • Arigatō.
  Hirano-san 03-4843-3311, Matsumoto-san 0472-63-9445

Page 20 Put it all together

1 *a* Iie, Airurando-jin desu; *b* Igirisu desu; *c* Iie, kaishain desu; *d* Watashi wa shufu desu; *e* 416-9227 desu.

2 *a* O-namae wa?; *b* O-shigoto wa?; *c* O-kuni wa?; *d* Kaisha no denwa bangō wa?

3 Shitsurei desu ga, o-kuni wa Amerika desu ka. Iie, Amerika ja arimasen. Igirisu desu. Sō desu ka. Rondon desu ka. Hai, sō desu. Ikeda-san wa? Watashi wa Yokohama desu. Kaisha mo Yokohama desu ka. Iie, kaisha wa Tōkyō desu.

Page 21 Now you're talking!

1 • Shitsurei desu ga, Amerika-jin desu ka.
  ◆ **Iie, Amerika-jin ja arimasen. Igirisu-jin desu.**

• Sō desu ka. Rondon desu ka.
◆ **Iie, Yōku desu.**
• A, Yōku desu ka. Shitsurei desu ga, gakusei desu ka.
◆ **Hai, sō desu. Gakusei desu.**

2 • Shitsurei desu ga, o-kuni wa dochira desu ka.
  ◆ **Igirisu desu.**
  • Sō desu ka. Rondon desu ka.
  ◆ **Hai, sō desu.**
  • Sō desu ka. Watashi wa Hashimoto desu. O-namae wa?
  ◆ **Watashi wa Fairlie desu.**
  • Fairlie-san, o-shigoto wa?
  ◆ **Enjinia desu. Hashimoto-san wa?**
  • Watashi desu ka. Watashi wa isha desu.

3 • Shitsurei desu ga, o-namae wa?
  ◆ **your family name + desu.**
  • O-kuni wa?
  ◆ **your country + desu.**
  • O-shigoto wa?
  ◆ **your occupation + desu.**
  • O-denwa bangō wa?
  ◆ **your phone number + desu.**
  • Hai, arigatō gozaimasu.

Page 22 Quiz

1 -jin; *2* shigoto; *3* ichi; *4* Pari; *5* no; *6* o-kuni wa?; *7* ka; *8* female; *9* gakusei ja arimasen; *10* your company phone number

Unit 3

Pages 24 & 25 Meeting friends and introducing another person

2 • Honda-san?
  ◆ A, Ogawa-san desu ka. Ohayō gozaimasu! **Shibaraku desu ne.**
  • Sō desu ne! **O-genki desu ka.**
  ◆ **Hai, o-kage sama de.**

3
a • Ohayō gozaimasu.
  ◆ A, Ikeda-san. Ohayō.
  • Atsui desu ne.

◆ Ee, atsui desu ne.
b ● Kimura-san? Shibaraku desu ne.
◆ A, Yamada-san. Sō desu ne.
O-genki desu ka.
● Hai, o-kage sama de. Kyō wa
iya-na tenki desu ne.
◆ Ee, mushiatsui desu ne.
c ● Konnichiwa.
◆ A, konnichiwa. Kyō wa samui
desu ne.
● Ee, samui desu ne.
1c, 2a, 3b

5 ● Ogawa-san?
◆ Mori-san, ohayō gozaimasu.
● Ohayō gozaimasu.
◆ Go-shōkai shimasu. Mori-san,
kochira wa Tōkyō Ginkō no
Honda-san desu.
● Honda desu. Dōzo yoroshiku.
◆ Mori desu. Dōzo yoroshiku.

6 ● A, sensei, konnichiwa.
◆ Konnichiwa. Kyō wa samui **desu ne**.
● Sō desu ne. Go-shōkai **shimasu.**
Sensei, **kochira wa** Yamaguchi-san
desu.
◆ Yamaguchi desu. Dōzo yoroshiku.
● James desu. Dōzo yoroshiku.

Pages 26 & 27 Talking about other people and asking their age

2 ● Kochira wa **okusan** desu ka.
◆ Hai, sō desu. **Kanai** desu.
● Shitsurei desu ga, okusan mo
sensei desu ka.
◆ Hai, sō desu. **Kanai mo** Eigo no
sensei desu.

3 ● **Yamada-san no o-tomodachi
desu ka.**
◆ Hai, sō desu.
● O-tomodachi no o-namae wa?
◆ Yamaguchi Keiko desu.
● Yamaguchi-san desu ka.
He asks if she is Yamada-san's friend.

4 15 = jū-go; 16 = jū-roku; 17 = jū-nana;
18 = jū-hachi; 19 = jū-kyū

5 ● ni-jū, san-jū, yon-jū, go-jū, roku-jū,
nana-jū
● roku-jū go, roku-jū roku, roku-jū
nana, roku-jū hachi, roku-jū kyū

7 ● A! Tanaka-san desu ne.
◆ E? A, sō desu ne. Tanaka-san to …
● Tanaka-san to gārufurendo!
◆ Sō desu ne. Gārufurendo wa wakai
desu ne! O-ikutsu desu ka. Ni-jū
is-sai? ni-jū san-sai?
● Sō desu ne.Tanaka-san wa o-ikutsu
desu ka.
◆ Tanaka-san? Tanaka-san wa san-jū
go-sai desu yo.
● San-jū go-sai desu ka!
*a = girlfriend; b = 21 or 23; c = 35
gārufurendo = girlfriend*

Page 28 Put it all together

1 atsui; ii; samui; iyana

2 *a* Kochira wa Yamaha no Saitō-san
desu; *b* Okusan wa o-genki desu ka;
c Kanai no namae wa Keiko desu;
d Kyō wa iya-na tenki desu ne;
e Watashi mo sensei desu.

3 Tomodachi no Ogawa-san desu.
Jū-kyū sai desu. Gakusei desu.

Page 29 Now you're talking!

1 ● **Kochira wa go-shujin desu ka.**
◆ Hai, sō desu.
● **O-shigoto wa nan desu ka?**
◆ Kaishain desu.
● **O-ikutsu desu ka.**
◆ Yon-jū nana-sai desu.
● **Wakai desu ne.**

2 ● **Konnichiwa. Shibaraku desu ne.**
◆ Sō desu ne.
● **O-genki desu ka.**
◆ Hai, o-kage sama de. Genki desu.
● **Kyō wa mushiatsui desu ne.**
◆ Sō desu ne. Iya-na tenki desu ne.
● **Go-shōkai shimasu. Kochira wa
Yamaha no Suzuki-san desu.**
◆ Suzuki desu. Dōzo yoroshiku.

3 ● **Kyō wa atsui desu ne.**
   ◆ Sō desu ne. Atsui desu ne.
   ● **Okusan desu ka.**
   ◆ Iie, sō ja arimasen. Gārufurendo desu.

Page 30 Quiz
1 no; *2* 30 years old; *3* no; *4* pleased;
5 Yamashita-sensei; *7* no; *8* introduce someone

Unit 4
Pages 32 & 33 Ordering a drink in a coffee shop
2 ● Irasshaimase!
   ◆ Sumimasen!
   ● Hai, nani ni nasaimasu ka.
   ◆ **Chiizu sando** o kudasai.
   ● Hai, chiizu sando desu ne.
   ◆ Chiizu sando to … kōra o kudasai.
   ● Chiizu sando to kōra desu ne.
   ◆ Hai.
   Yamada-san orders a cheese sandwich first.

3 Drinks: *a coffee; b orange juice;*
   c lemon juice; d milk; e cocoa
   Food: *f hamburger; g ice cream;*
   h ham sandwich; i cheesecake; j toast

4 ● Irasshaimase. Nani ni nasaimasu ka.
   ◆ Tanaka-san wa?
   ● Sō desu ne. **Kōhii** o kudasai.
   ◆ Ishii-san wa?
   ● Hai, watashi wa **orenji jūsu** to **hamu sando**.
   ◆ Remon jūsu to hamu sando desu ne.
   ● Iie, remon jūsu ja arimasen. Orenji jūsu desu.
   ◆ Sumimasen. Orenji jūsu desu ne.

6 ● Sumimasen!
   ◆ Hai.
   ● Sore wa?
   ◆ Kore wa **chiizukēk**i desu.
   ● Sō desu ka. Kore wa?
   ◆ Sore wa appuru pai desu.
   ● Ja, kore o kudasai.

She orders 'this one' – apple pie.

7 ● Nani ni nasaimasu ka.
   ◆ Hamu sando **to** remon tii o kudasai.
   ● Watashi mo remon tii. Remon tii to aisu kuriimu **o** kudasai.
   ◆ **Watashi wa** aisu kuriimu to kōra o kudasai.
   ● Hai. Remon tii o **futatsu**, hamu sando o hitotsu, aisu kuriimu o futatsu, kōra o **hitotsu** desu ne.
   ◆ Hai, sō desu.
   They order two lemon teas, one ham sandwich, two ice creams and one coke.

Pages 34 & 35 Offering someone a drink and accepting or refusing
2 ● Ohayō gozaimasu.
   ◆ Ohayō gozaimasu.
   ● **O-cha o dōzo.**
   ◆ Hai, arigatō gozaimasu.
   ● Kyō wa samui desu ne.
   ◆ Sō desu ne. Samui desu ne.
   ● **O-cha mō sukoshi ikaga desu ka.**
   ◆ **Hai, onegai shimasu.**
   ● **Dōzo.**
   Yes – he has another cup of o-cha.

3 ● Yamada-san, **kōhii** wa, ikaga desu ka?
   ◆ Ii desu ne. Hai, onegai shimasu.
   ● Dōzo. **Kuriimu** wa?
   ◆ Iie, kekkō desu.
   Yamada-san was offered coffee with cream; she had coffee but no cream.

4 Kōhii wa ikaga desu ka; Kōcha wa ikaga desu ka; Mō sukoshi ikaga desu ka.

6 ● Fujie-san, konbanwa. Biiru wa ikaga desu ka.
   ◆ Hai, onegai shimasu. Arigatō.
   ● **Kanpai!**
   ◆ **Kanpai!**
   ● **Oishii desu ne!**

7 ● Sumimasen!
   ◆ Hai.

- Yakitori o kudasai.
- Hai, yakitori desu. Dōzo.
- Dōmo. Itadakimasu.
- Itadakimasu. Yakitori wa oishii desu ne.
- Hmm, sō desu ne. Fujie-san, biiru wa? Mō sukoshi ikaga desu ka.
- Iie, kekkō desu.
- O-sake wa?
- Iie, mō kekkō desu.
- Sō desu ne. Watashi mo. Sumimasen!
- O-kanjō o onegai shimasu.
- Hai, dōzo. Arigatō gozaimashita.
- Gochisō sama deshita.
- Gochisō sama.

No she didn't.

Page 36 Put it all together

1 *a* Iie, kekkō desu; *b* Arigatō; *c* Yakitori o kudasai.

2 *a* Kōcha o yottsu kudasai; *b* Kōhii to tōsuto o kudasai; *c* Yakitori wa oishii desu; *d* Kore wa appuru pai desu.

3 *a* Kōhii o futatsu to chiizukēki o hitotsu kudasai; *b* Kōcha o mittsu to hamu sando o futatsu kudasai; *c* Kōra o yottsu to aisu kuriimu o mittsu kudasai.

Page 37 Now you're talking!

1 • Sumimasen.
   ◆ **Hai, nani ni nasaimasu ka.**
   • Aisu kōhii o futatsu to chiizu sando o hitotsu kudasai.

2 • Kōhii wa ikaga desu ka.
   ◆ **Hai, onegai shimasu.**
   • Dōzo.
   ◆ **Arigatō.**
   • Kuriimu wa?
   ◆ **Iie, kekkō desu.**

3 • **Irasshaimase!**
   ◆ Biiru o kudasai.
   • **Hai, biiru desu ne. Dōzo.**
   ◆ Arigatō.

4 • Biiru wa ikaga desu ka.
   ◆ **Hai, onegai shimasu.**
   • Dōzo.
   ◆ **Dōmo.**
   • Kanpai!
   ◆ **Kanpai!**
   • Hai, yakitori o dōzo.
   ◆ **Dōmo. Itadakimasu.**
   • O-kanjō o onegai shimasu.
   ◆ **Gochisō sama deshita.**

Page 38 Quiz

1 the people who work in restaurants, izakaya, kissaten as you enter; *2* rice wine; *3* kōhii o futatsu to aisu kuriimu o hitotsu kudasai; *4* after a meal as a set phrase of thanks; *5* itadakimasu; *6* sumimasen; *7* kanpai!; *8* izakaya; *9* sore o kudasai; *10* yes

Chekkupointo 1

Pages 39 – 42

1 • Shigoto desu ka. Yasumi desu ka.
   ◆ **Yasumi desu.**
   • Yasumi desu ka. Shitsurei desu ga, kochira wa go-shujin desu ka.
   ◆ Iie, chigaimasu. Tomodachi desu.
   • Sō desu ka. Amerika-jin desu ka.
   ◆ **Tomodachi wa Amerika-jin** desu ga, watashi wa **Igirisu-jin** desu.
   • Sō desu ka. O-shigoto wa?
   ◆ **Kaishain** desu.
   • Kaishain desu ka. Sumimasen, o-namae wa?
   ◆ Ann desu. Ann Wilson desu.
   • Hai, dōmo arigatō gozaimashita.

2 • O-kuni wa dochira desu ka. Igirisu desu ka.
   ◆ Sukottorando desu.
   • Sō desu ka. Ii desu ne. Shitsurei desu ga, o-namae wa?
   ◆ Jenny Davis desu.
   • Jenny-san desu ka. Watashi wa Takeshi desu. Saito Takeshi desu. Dōzo yoroshiku.

- Dōzo yoroshiku.
- Shigoto desu ka.
- Iie, shigoto ja arimasen. Watashi wa gakusei desu.
- A, gakusei-san desu ka. Doko desu ka Tōkyō desu ka.
- Hai, Tōkyō desu. Takeshi-san mo gakusei desu.
- Hai, sō desu.
- Tōkyō desu ka.
- Iie, Kyōto desu. Anō ... Jenny-san wa o-ikutsu desu ka.
- Jū-kyū sai desu.
- Jū-kyū sai desu ka. Watashi wa ni-jū ni sai desu.
Takeshi – Japanese; 22; Kyoto. Jenny – Scottish; 19; Tokyo

3
- Kōhii, jūsu, o-cha, sandoitchi, ikaga desu ka.
- Sumimasen, kōhii o kudasai. Sore kara, hamu sando.
- Hai, kōhii to hamu sando desu ne. Dōzo.
- Jenny-san wa?
- Watashi wa orenji jūsu. A, chiizu sando mo kudasai.
- Hai, orenji jūsu to chiizu sando desu ne.
Takeshi: coffee and a ham sandwich; Jenny: orange juice and a cheese sandwich

5 Burajiru (*Brazil*) wa 0055 desu. Indo (*India*) wa 0091 desu. Mekishiko (*Mexico*) wa 0052 desu. Nepāru (*Nepal*) wa 00977 desu. Oranda (*Holland*) wa 0031 desu. Suēden (*Sweden*) wa 0046 desu. Tai (*Thailand*) wa 0066 desu. Maruta (*Malta*) wa 00356 desu.

6 *a* Dōzo yoroshiku; *b* Shibaraku desu ne; *c* Kanpai!; *d* Itadakimasu; *e* Shitsurei shimasu; *f* Arigatō; *g* Konbanwa.

7 *a* O-namae wa?
  b Denwa bangō wa nan-ban desu ka.

c O-ikutsu desu ka.
d O-shigoto wa?

8 *c; b; d; a*

9 *a* rei; *b* shufu; *c* shigoto; *d* kirei; *e* atsui; *f* nani.

10 Across: *1* O-cha wa **ikaga** desu ka; *4* Iie, watashi wa gakusei ja **arimasen**; *6* Kōhii o hitotsu to kōra o futatsu kudasai; *7* Yamada-**san** wa o-ikutsu desu ka; *9* **Kyō** wa atsui desu ne!; *10* Amerika-**jin** desu ka.

Down: *1* **Iyana** tenki desu ne; *2* Dōmo **arigatō**; *3* **Denwa** bangō wa nan-ban desu ka; *5* **Are** wa appuru pai desu ka; *7* Ikura desu ka. **Sen** en desu; *8* Kyō wa **nan**yōbi desu ka; *9* O-namae wa nan desu **ka**.

Unit 5

Pages 44 & 45 Asking where something is and asking for help to understand

2
- Mitsukoshi Depāto wa doko desu ka.
- Wakarimasen. Guriin Hoteru wa koko desu ne.
- Hai.
- Sore kara ... a, yūbinkyoku wa koko desu ne.
- Doko desu ka.
- Koko desu.
- Sō desu ne. Tōkyō eki wa soko desu ne.
- Sō desu ne. Yūbinkyoku ... Tōkyō eki ... a! Mitsukoshi Depāto! Asoko desu!
hoteru = hotel

3
- Sumimasen. Tōkyō eki wa **doko desu ka**.
- Watashi mo **wakarimasen**.
- Sō desu ka. Dōmo **sumimasen**.

Sumimasen. Tōkyō eki wa **doko desu ka.**
- A, Tōkyō eki desu ka. **Asoko desu.**
- Dōmo arigatō.

4 ● Sumimasen.
- Hai.
- Sakura Hoteru wa doko desu ka.
- Sakura Hoteru ne. Asoko desu yo.
- Sumimasen, mō ichido onegai shimasu.
- Hai, Sakura Hoteru wa asoko desu.
- Sō desu ka. Arigatō.

Sakura Hotel is over there.

6 *a* true; *b* false; *c* false; *d* true

7 ● Sumimasen ga …
- Hai.
- Kōen wa doko desu ka.
- Kōen desu ka. Kōen wa eki no ushiro desu yo.
- Sumimasen. Motto yukkuri, onegai shimasu.
- A, sumimasen. Eki wa asoko desu.
- Hai.
- Kōen wa eki no ushiro desu.
- Hai, arigatō.

The park is behind the station.

Pages 46 & 47 Talking about where you live and work

2 ● O-sumai wa dochira desu ka. Rondon desu ka.
- Iie, Rondon ja arimasen. Redingu desu.
- Sumimasen, mō ichido. Re …?
- Redingu. Rondon no chikaku desu.
- A sō desu ka.

The tourist is from Reading.

3 ● Sō desu ka. Atarashii uchi wa doko desu ka.
- Yokohama desu.
- Yokohama desu ka. Apāto desu ka.
- Hai, apāto desu.

apāto = apartment/flat

4 ● Saitō-san no uchi wa doko desu ka.
- Nakano desu. Eki no chikaku desu.
- Ii desu ne. Apāto desu ka.
- Hai, atarashii apāto desu.

Nakano; near station; flat; new

6 ● O-tsutome wa dochira desu ka? Ima mo Asahi Ginkō desu ka.
- Iie, chigaimasu. Ima wa Hitachi desu.
- Hitachi desu ka. Ii desu ne. Kaisha wa doko desu ka. Kono chikaku desu ka.
- Hai, sō desu. Ano biru desu.

She is close to the office.

7 ● Takeshi-san no o-shigoto wa? Sensei desu ka.
- Iie, chigaimasu yo. Sensei ja arimasen. Kaishain desu.
- Sō desu ka. Dono kaisha desu ka.
- Kiku Enjinia ringu desu.
- Ii desu ne. Doko desu ka, kaisha wa? Kono chikaku desu ka.
- Hai, sono depāto no tonari desu.

a true; *b* true; *c* false

Page 48 Put it all together

1 *a* Eki no mae desu; *b* Iie, ushiro desu; *c* Yokohama desu; *d* Hoteru wa ano biru desu; *e* Iie, chigaimasu, Yokohama desu.

2 *a* O-sumai wa dochira desu ka; *b* Kissaten wa depāto no naka desu; *c* Mō ichido onegai shimasu; *d* Dono biru desu ka.

3 ● Tanaka-san no kaisha wa doko desu ka.
- Kaisha desu ka. Sono biru desu.
- Dono biru desu ka.
- Sono ginkō no tonari desu.
- Sō desu ka. Tanaka-san no uchi wa doko desu ka. Tanaka-san no uchi?
- Wakarimasen.
- Watashi mo wakarimasen.

Page 49 Now you're talking!

1 ● Ohayō gozaimasu. Sumimasen.
  Yūbinkyoku wa doko desu ka
  ◆ Ano depāto no tonari desu.
  ● Mō ichido, onegai shimasu.
  ◆ Hai, depāto no tonari desu.
  ● Dōmo arigatō.

2 ● Sumimasen.
  ◆ Hai.
  ● Hibiya Kōen wa asoko desu ka.
  ◆ Iie, chigaimasu. Asoko desu. Ano
    hoteru no ushiro desu.
  ● Motto yukkuri, onegai shimasu.
  ◆ Asoko desu. Ano hoteru no ushiro
    desu.
  ● Sō desu ka. Dōmo sumimasen.

3 ● O-tsutome wa dochira desu ka.
  ◆ Ginkō desu.
  ● Ginkō wa kono chikaku desu ka.
  ◆ Hai, ano biru desu.
  ● O-sumai wa dochira desu ka.
  ◆ Kamakura desu.
  ● Kamakura wa doko desu ka.
    Tōkyō no chikaku desu ka.
  ◆ Hai, sō desu.

Page 50 Quiz

1 there; *2* kōen; *3* wakarimasen;
4 Mitsukoshi Department Store;
5 if you hadn't quite understood what
they had said – to speak more slowly;
6 sō ja arimasen; *7* kono biru, this
building – sono biru, that building;
8 mō ichido, onegai shimasu; *9* police
office; *10* wrong

Unit 6

**Pages 52 & 53 Finding out about
facilities and asking where someone is**

2   furonto = front desk/reception;
    toire = toilet; robii = lobby; pūru
    = swimming pool; dorai kuriiningu
    = dry cleaning; bā = bar; raunji =
    lounge; erebētā = lift/elevator

3 ● Kono chikaku ni, ginkō wa arimasu
    ka.
  ◆ Ginkō wa asoko desu. Depāto no
    tonari ni arimasu.
  ● Hai, arigatō.
  Yes, there's a bank.

4 ● Sumimasen.
  ◆ Atarashii hoteru no namae wa Nyū
    Kyōto Hoteru desu ka.
  ● Hai, sō desu.
  ◆ Sono hoteru ni, **pūru** wa arimasu ka.
  ● Hai, pūru ga arimasu.
  ◆ Sō desu ka. **Dorai kuriiningu** wa
    arimasu ka.
  ● Sumimasen, hoteru no naka ni
    dorai kuriiningu wa arimasen.
    Hoteru no chikaku ni arimasu.
  ◆ Sō desu ka.
  ● Hai.
  ◆ **Bā** wa arimasu ka.
  ● Hai, bā ga arimasu.
  ◆ Ii desu ne.

6 ● Tanaka-san wa doko ni imasu ka.
  ◆ Wakarimasen!
  ● Sō desu ka. Pūru ni imasu ka.
  ◆ Iie, pūru ni imasen.
  ● Ja, kissaten ni imasu ka.
  ◆ Tanaka-san? Iie, kissaten ni imasen
    yo.
  ● Asoko ni hito ga takusan imasu ne.
    A!
  ◆ Nan desu ka.
  ● Asoko desu. Tanaka-san wa asoko
    ni imasu yo.
  ◆ Ā, sō desu ne. Bā ni imasu ne.
  Tanaka-san is in the bar.

7 ● Asoko ni hito ga takusan **imasu** ne.
  ◆ Sō desu ne. Nani ga **arimasu** ka.
  ● A! Kyō wa, matsuri ga **arimasu**.
  ◆ Sō desu ka. A! Asoko ni tomodachi
    ga **imasu**.

8 ● Kono chikaku ni, kissaten wa
    arimasu ka.
  ◆ Yamada-san wa bā ni imasu ka.

Pages 54 & 55 Understanding how to find a place and when it's open

2 ● Sumimasen.
  ◆ Hai.
  ● Anō, Yamashita Kōen wa doko ni arimasu ka.
  ◆ Yamashita Kōen desu ka. Ēto, massugu itte, migi desu. Yamashita Kōen wa migi ni arimasu.
  ● Dōmo arigatō.
  ◆ Iie.
  The park is to the right.

3 ● Sumimasen, kono chikaku ni kissaten wa arimasu ka.
  ◆ Kissaten desu ka. Hai, kōen no naka ni arimasu yo. Ēto … Massugu itte, hidari desu. Pūru no tonari ni arimasu.
  ● Dōmo sumimasen.
  ◆ Iie.
  The coffee shop is in the park. Go straight ahead, then left, it's next to the pool.

6 ● Hai! … Pūru desu ka. Hai, Shimizu Pūru ga arimasu … Iie, mainichi ja arimasen. Suiyōbi wa yasumi desu. … Hai! … Sakura matsuri desu ka. Hai, Ueno Kōen ni arimasu ne. Doyōbi kara desu … A, sō desu ne, ashita kara desu. Ashita wa doyōbi desu ne … Hai! … Matsuya Depāto desu ka. Hai, chikaku ni arimasu … Hai, kyō wa aite imasu. Yasumi wa getsuyōbi desu.
  a closed on Wednesday; b from Saturday; c closed on Monday

7 ● Ohayō gozaimasu, Kimura Dorai Kuriiningu desu … Hai, kyō wa aite imasu. Mainichi aite imasu … Hai, dōmo arigatō gozaimashita.
  ◆ Hai, supōtsu sentā desu … Sumimasen ga, ashita wa yasumi desu … Hai, kayōbi desu ne.

Kayōbi wa yasumi desu. Suiyōbi kara aite imasu … Hai, arigatō gozaimashita.
a true; b true; c false

Page 56 Put it all together

1 a exit; b yes – women; c entrance

Page 57 Now you're talking!

1 ● **Sumimasen. Kono chikaku ni kankō annaijo wa arimasu ka.**
  ◆ Hai, arimasu. Massugu itte, hidari desu.
  ● **Massugu itte, hidari desu ne. Dōmo arigatō.**
  ◆ Iie.

2 ● **Kono chikaku ni pūru wa arimasu ka.**
  ◆ Hai, kono chikaku ni supōtsu sentā ga arimasu. Supōtsu sentā no naka ni pūru ga arimasu.
  ● **Ashita wa aite imasu ka.**
  ◆ Hai, aite imasu.
  ● **Yasumi wa nan-yōbi desu ka**
  ◆ Getsuyōbi desu.
  ● **Arigatō gozaimasu.**

3 ● **Hito ga takusan imasu ne. Nani ga arimasu ka.**
  ◆ Kyō wa matsuri desu.
  ● **Sō desu ka. Ashita mo arimasu ka.**
  ◆ Hai, kyō mo ashita mo arimasu. Yamashita Kōen no naka desu.
  ● **Yamashita Kōen wa doko ni arimasu ka.**
  ◆ Hoteru kara migi desu. Sore kara, massugu desu. Migi ni arimasu.
  ● **Dōmo, arigatō.**

Page 58 Quiz

1 migi = right, hidari = left; 2 person; 3 Denwa wa arimasu ka; 4 Kyō wa kin-yōbi desu; 5 festival; 6 nanyōbi; 7 tourist information centre; 8 sakura

Unit 7

Pages 60 & 61 Understanding prices in yen and asking for items

2 ni-hyaku, yon-hyaku, kyū-hyaku san-ju, go-hyaku go-jū, hyaku ni-jū, nana-hyaku hachi-jū.

3

a • Sumimasen, ringo wa ikura desu ka.
   ◆ Ringo desu ka. Hitotsu, ni-hyaku yon-jū en desu.
   • Ni-hyaku yon-jū en desu ka!

b • Irasshaimase!
   ◆ Sumimasen. Kono painappuru wa ikura desu ka.
   • Hap-pyaku kyū-jū en desu. Painappuru wa hap-pyaku kyū-jū en desu.

c • Kono meron wa ii desu ne. Ikura desu ka.
   ◆ Kyō, meron wa ni-sen nana-hyaku en desu.
   • E!? Ni-sen nana-hyaku en desu ka!!

d • Hai, ringo to painappuru to tomato to meron desu ne. Ēto, yon-sen hyaku en desu.
   ◆ Hai, Yon-sen hyaku en.
   • Dōmo arigatō gozaimashita.
   a ¥240; *b* ¥890; *c* ¥2700; *d* ¥4100

5 • Sumimasen, sandoitchi wa arimasu ka.
   ◆ Hai, gozaimasu. **Hamu sando, chiizu sando, mikkusu sando** ga gozaimasu.
   • Ja, mikkusu sando o kudasai.
   ◆ Hai.
   • Sore kara … a, **appuru jūsu** wa arimasu ka.
   ◆ Sumimasen. Appuru jūsu wa gozaimasen. **Orenji jūsu** ga gozaimasu ga.
   • Ja, orenji jūsu o onegai shimasu. Sore kara, kono **shinbun** mo.
   ◆ 'Japan Times' desu ne.

• Hai. Zenbu de ikura desu ka.
◆ Hai, zenbu de ¥1250 de gozaimasu.
• ¥1250 desu ne. Hai.
◆ Dōmo arigatō gozaimashita.
Mikkusu sando; orenji jūsu; shinbun

6 • Kōhii, sandoitchi, aisu kuriimu wa ikaga desu ka.
   ◆ Sumimasen, **kōhii** o kudasai.
   • Hai, kōhii desu ne.
   ◆ Sore kara, poteto chippu wa arimasu ka.
   • Gozaimasu.
   ◆ Ja, onegai shimasu.
   • Hai, ¥720 de gozaimasu.
   ◆ Hai.
   • Hai, ¥280 no o-tsuri de gozaimasu.
   Poteto chippu = crisps; ¥280

Pages 62 & 63 Coping in the post office and the department store

2 • Sumimasen, kono tegami wa Igirisu made ikura desu ka.
   ◆ Kōkūbin desu ka.
   • Hai, kōkūbin de, onegai shimasu.
   ◆ ¥220 desu.
   • Sumimasen, mō ichido onegai shimasu.
   ◆ Hai. ¥220 desu.
   • Ja, ¥220 kitte o san-mai kudasai.
   ◆ San-mai desu ne. Hai, dōzo. ¥660 desu.
   England; ¥220; three

3 • Kono tegami wa Amerika **made** ikura desu ka.
   ◆ **Kōkūbin** desu ka.
   • Hai, sō desu.
   ◆ **¥220** desu.
   • Sore kara, ¥100 kitte o **go-mai** kudasai.
   ◆ Hai, dōzo. **Zenbu de** ¥720 desu.

5 • Sumimasen, **sore o misete kudasai**.
   ◆ Kono kamera desu ne. Dōzo.
   • A, **chotto ōkii desu ne. Motto chiisai no wa arimasu ka**.

- Hai, gozaimasu. Kochira wa ikaga desu ka.
- Kono kamera wa ii desu ne. Ikura desu ka.
- ¥30,700 de gozaimasu.
- ¥30,700 en desu ka. Hai, **kore onegai shimasu.**

Camera: ¥30,700.

6 • Ikaga desu ka.
- Sō desu ne … kono kutsu wa ii desu ga … chotto ōkii desu ne. Motto chiisai no wa arimasu ka.
- Saizu wa?
- Ni-jū san wa arimasu ka.
- Ni-jū san … Hai, gozaimasu. Dōzo.
- A, ii desu ne. Ja, kore onegai shimasu.

a false; *b* true; *c* true

7 • ¥120 kitte o ni-mai kudasai.
- Motto chiisai kamera wa arimasu ka.
- Furansu no kutsu wa chotto takai desu ne.

Page 64 Put it all together

1 *a* altogether; *b* a little small; *c* by airmail; *d* change; *e* how much?; *f* a cheaper one; *g* do you have?

2 ¥85 kitte o ni-mai kudasai; Hagaki o san-mai kudasai; ringo o futatsu kudasai; appuru jūsu o kudasai; poteto chippu o kudasai.

3 Sumimasen, sono beruto o misete kudasai. Kono Furansu no beruto desu ka. Hai, dōzo. Ikura desu ka. ¥7600? Chotto takai desu ne. Motto yasui no wa arimasu ka. Hai. Kono beruto wa ¥3,700 desu. Itaria no beruto desu. Ii desu ne. Ja, kono Itaria no beruto o kudasai.

4 ¥6820

Page 65 Now you're talking!

1 • **Kono tegami wa Igirisu made ikura desu ka.**
- Kōkūbin desu ka.
- **Hai. Kōkūbin de onegai shimasu.**
- ¥140 desu.
- **¥140 kitte o san-mai kudasai.**
- Dōzo. ¥420 desu.
- **Dōmo arigatō gozaimasu.**

2 • Irasshaimase.
- **Ano tokei o misete kudasai.**
- Hai, dōzo.
- **Chotto chiisai desu ne. Motto ōkii no wa arimasu ka.**
- Hai, gozaimasu.
- **Ii desu ne. Ikura desu ka.**
- ¥8500 de gozaimasu.
- **Ja. Kore onegai shimasu.**

3 • **Appuru jūsu to chiizu sando o kudasai.**
- Hai, dōzo.
- **Japan Times wa arimasu ka.**
- Sumimasen. Japan Times wa gozaimasen.
- **Zenbu de ikura desu ka.**
- ¥730 de gozaimasu.
- **¥1000 desu.**
- Hai, ¥270 no o-tsuri de gozaimasu.

Page 66 Quiz

1 san-mai; *2* it's not available; *3* ¥10,000; *4* read; *5* post office; *6* yes; *7* sono kamera o misete kudasai; *8* kōkūbin de, onegai shimasu

Chekkupointo 2

Pages 67 – 70

1 *a* **Yamashita Kōen B**
- Sumimasen, Yamashita Kōen wa doko ni arimasu ka.
- Yamashita Kōen desu ka. Hai. Massugu itte, hidari ni arimasu.
- Sumimasen, mō ichido onegai shimasu.

- ◆ Hai, massugu itte, hidari ni arimasu.
- ● Hai, dōmo arigatō.

b **Seibu Depāto C**
- ● Sumimasen, Seiyū Depāto wa kono chikaku ni arimasu ka.
- ◆ Seiyū Depāto desu ka. Iie, arimasen. Seibu ja arimasen ka.
- ● A, Seibu desu ka. Sumimasen.
- ◆ Iie. Seibu Depāto wa asoko desu yo.
- ● Doko desu ka.
- ◆ Asoko desu. Hoteru no tonari desu.
- ● A, sō desu ka! Dōmo arigatō!

c **Tōkyō eki A**
- ● Sumimasen, Tōkyō eki wa doko desu ka. Kono chikaku desu ka.
- ◆ Tōkyō eki desu ka. Hai. Massugu itte, migi desu. Tōkyō eki wa hidari ni arimasu.
- ● Massugu itte, migi desu ne. Dōmo arigatō.

2
a Kōen no **naka** ni pūru ga arimasu.
b **Ginkō** wa hoteru no mukai ni arimasu.
c Yūbinkyoku wa eki no tonari ni arimasu.
d Kankō annaijo wa **eki** no mae ni arimasu.

3 Tomato wa san-byaku nana-jū en desu. Ringo wa go-hyaku roku-jū en desu. Banana wa ni-hyaku hachi-jū en desu ne. Painappuru wa nana-hyaku roku-jū en desu. Meron wa ni-sen kyū-hyaku hachi-jū en desu. Miruku wa hyaku san-jū en desu. Poteto chippu wa hyaku roku-jū en desu. Ii desu ka. Ja, zenbu de … go-sen ni-hyaku yon-jū en desu ne.
tomato ¥370; apple ¥560; banana ¥280; pineapple ¥760; melon ¥2980; milk ¥130; crisps ¥160; total ¥5240

4 ● Sumimasen!
- ◆ Hai.
- ● Pūru wa doko desu ka.
- ◆ Hoteru no pūru desu ka. Massugu itte, hidari desu.
- ● Ima aite imasu ka.
- ◆ Hai, mainichi aite imasu.
- ● Arigatō. Sore kara, hoteru no chikaku ni yūbinkyoku wa arimasu ka.
- ◆ Arimasu ga, kyō wa yasumi desu.
- ● Yasumi desu ka.
- ◆ Hai, nichiyōbi desu ne.
- ● A, sō desu ka. Kyō wa nichiyōbi desu ne. Dōmo sumimasen.
a true; *b* true; *c* false; *d* true

5 *a* kono; *b* biru; *c* motto; *d* en; *e* migi

6 *a* Chigaimasu; *b* Wakarimasen; *c* Motto yukkuri, onegai shimasu; *d* Chotto chiisai desu; *e* Mō ichido onegai shimasu; *f* Misete kudasai.

7 getsuyōbi; mokuyōbi; kinyōbi; kayōbi; nichiyōbi; doyōbi. The answer is suiyōbi.

8 *a* yūbinkyoku; *b* depāto; *c* izakaya; *d* kōban; *e* eki no kiosuku; *f* hoteru

9 *a* bottom picture – right door; *b* top picture – left door; *c* top picture – right door; *d* bottom picture – left door

Unit 8

Page 72 Finding a hotel room

2 ● Irasshaimase.
- ◆ **Konban, heya wa arimasu ka.**
- ● Hai, gozaimasu. Shinguru desu ka. Tsuin desu ka.
- ◆ **Shinguru o onegai shimasu. Ip-paku ikura desu ka.**
- ● Ip-paku ¥10,500 de gozaimasu.
- ◆ Ja, onegai shimasu.
He wants a single room.

3 ● Irasshaimase.
◆ Sumimasen. Konban heya wa arimasu ka.
● Shinguru wa gozaimasen ga …
◆ Sō desu ka. Tsuin wa?
● Tsuin ga gozaimasu ga.
◆ Ip-paku ikura desu ka.
● ¥20,000 de gozaimasu.
◆ Ja, onegai shimasu.
● Nan-paku de gozaimasu ka.
◆ Ni-haku onegai shimasu.
a two nights; *b* ¥20,000;
c twin room.

Page 73 Booking ahead by phone

2 ● Hai, Miyako Hoteru de gozaimasu.
◆ A, moshi moshi. Yoyaku o onegai shimasu.
● Hai, itsu deshō ka.
◆ Ashita desu. Suiyōbi desu.
● Ashita desu ka. Sumimasen, ashita wa chotto …
◆ Arimasen ka.
● Hai, sumimasen.
She wants to reserve a room for tomorrow. The hotel is full.

3 ● Hai, Yamanaka Hoteru de gozaimasu.
◆ Moshi moshi. Ano … yoyaku o onegai shimasu.
● Hai, itsu deshō ka.
◆ 3-gatsu 23-nichi ni heya wa arimasu ka.
● Shinguru deshō ka. Tsuin deshō ka.
◆ Shinguru o onegai shimasu.
● Hai, gozaimasu. Ip-paku de gozaimasu ka.
◆ Hai, ip-paku o onegai shimasu.
● Dewa, o-namae o onegai shimasu.
◆ Hai, Ikeda desu. Ikeda Haruo desu.

● Hai, Yamanaka Hoteru de gozaimasu.
◆ Sumimasen ga, ano … yoyaku o onegai shimasu.

● Hai, dōzo. Itsu desu ka.
◆ 5-gatsu tsuitachi to futsuka.
● Ni-haku desu ne.
◆ Hai, sō desu.
● Shinguru deshō ka. Tsuin deshō ka.
◆ Tsuin o onegai shimasu.
● Hai, gozaimasu.
◆ Ja, onegai shimasu.
● O-namae wa?
◆ Wada desu. Wada Shūsaku.
Ikeda-san: March 23; single room
Wada-san: May 1 and 2; twin room

Pages 74 & 75 Checking in at reception and asking about facilities

2 ● Irasshaimase.
◆ Ano … yoyaku shimashita ga …
● Hai, o-namae wa?
◆ Fujimura Yoko desu.
● Fujimura san … Hai, washitsu desu ne.
◆ Hai, sō desu.
● Dōzo, o-namae to go-jūsho o onegai shimasu.
Japanese-style room. (washitsu).

3 ● O-heya wa go-kai desu. Dōzo, kochira e.
◆ Ano … resutoran to bā wa nan-gai desu ka.
● Resutoran wa ni-kai to kyū-kai desu. Bā mo kyū-kai desu.
◆ Kono hoteru ni, washitsu mo arimasu ka.
● Hai, yōshitsu mo washitsu mo arimasu. San-gai no heya wa zenbu washitsu desu.
◆ Sō desu ka. Furo wa?
● Hai, o-furo mo san-gai desu.
resutoran – restaurant, 2nd floor and 9th floor; furo – Japanese style bath, 3rd floor; washitsu – Japanese-style rooms, 3rd floor; bā – bar, 9th floor

4 ● Irasshaimase.
◆ Yoyaku shimashita ga …
● Hai, o-namae wa?

- Yamada Akiko desu.
- Hai, kochira ni o-namae to go-jūsho to denwa bangō o onegai shimasu.
- Koko desu ka.
- Hai, onegai shimasu … Arigatō gozaimashita. O-heya wa washitsu desu ne.
- Hai, washitsu o onegai shimasu.
- Dewa, dōzo kochira e. O-heya wa san-gai desu.
  a true; b true; c false; d false

6
- Sumimasen, shokuji tsuki desu ka.
- Hai, ni-shoku tsuki desu ga. Chōshoku to yūshoku desu.
- Ii desu ne. Furo wa? Furo tsuki desu ka.
- Heya ni wa o-furo wa arimasen ga, shawā ga arimasu.
- Shawā ne.
- Hai, sore kara heya wa zenbu terebi tsuki desu.
- Sumimasen ga, kono hoteru ni fakkusu wa arimasu ka.
- Sumimasen ga, ima fakkusu wa arimasen.
- Sō desu ka.
  The hotel includes meals, has TVs in all rooms, does not have a fax, does not have baths but showers.

7
- Ni-shoku tsuki desu ka.
- Shawā wa arimasu ka.
- Washitsu to yōshitsu wa arimasu ka.

Page 76 Put it all together

1 *a* Are meals included?; *b* Hello?; *c* How many nights?; *d* How about breakfast?; *e* Is it a Japanese-style room?; *f* It's on the fourth floor; *g* When for?

2 *a* Tsuin o onegai shimasu; *b* Shawā tsuki desu ka; *c* 6-gatsu 16 nichi ni heya wa arimasu ka; *d* Shokuji tsuki desu ka.

3
- Moshi moshi. Yoyaku o onegai shimasu.
- Hai, yoyaku desu ne. Itsu deshō ka.
- 18-nichi desu.
- Kinyōbi desu ne. Shinguru desu ka. Tsuin desu ka.
- Shinguru o onegai shimasu. Ip-paku ikura desu ka.
- Ip-paku ¥9800 desu.
- Ja, onegai shimasu.

4 Christmas Day = jū-ni gatsu ni-jū go-nichi.
New Year's Day = ichi-gatsu tsuitachi.

Page 77 Now you're talking!

1
- Irasshaimase.
- **Konban heya wa arimasu ka.**
- Shinguru desu ka. Daburu desu ka.
- **Shinguru o onegai shimasu.**
- Hai, nan-paku desu ka.
- **Ip-paku o onegai shimasu.**
- Hai, gozaimasu.
- **Ip-paku ikura desu ka.**
- ¥12,000 de gozaimasu.
- **Hai, onegai shimasu.**

2
- Irasshaimase.
- **Yoyaku shimashita. Namae wa John Graham desu.**
- Graham-san desu ne. Hai, daburu desu ne.
- **Iie, chigaimasu, shinguru desu.**
- Sō desu ka. Shitsurei shimashita. Shinguru, san-paku desu ne.
- **Iie, ni-haku desu.**
- Shitsurei shimashita, o-namae o mō ichido onegai shimasu.
- **Namae wa John Graham desu.**
- A, John Graham-san desu ne. Dōmo shitsurei shimashita. Shinguru, ni-haku no yoyaku desu ne.
- **Hai, sō desu.**

Page 78 Quiz

1 on the phone; *2* yes; *3* in a ryokan (Japanese-style inn); *4* April 1;

5 the number of nights; *6* washitsu –
Japanese-style inn; *7* have a bath;
8 hatsuka.

Unit 9

Pages 80 & 81 Finding out train times and buying tickets

2 • Sumimasen. **Tsugi no** Nagoya yuki
wa nan-ji desu ka.
  ♦ **Hachi-ji han** desu.
  • **Hachi-ji han** desu ka. Hai.
    Sore kara, Nagoya wa **nan-ji ni**
    tsukimasu ka.
  ♦ Nagoya wa **jū-ji han** ni tsukimasu.
  • **Jū-ji han** desu ne. Arigatō.

3 • Sumimasen, ano … tsugi no Ōsaka
    yuki wa nan-ji desu ka.
  ♦ Ōsaka yuki desu ka. Tsugi no
    Ōsaka yuki wa ku-ji desu.
  • Ku-ji desu ne. Hai. Nan-ji ni
    tsukimasu ka.
  ♦ Jū-ni-ji ni tsukimasu. Ōsaka wa
    jū-ni-ji desu.
  • Arigatō.
  • Sumimasen, tsugi no Kyōto yuki
    desu ga. Nan-ji desu ka.
  ♦ Kyōto desu ka. Tsugi no Kyōto yuki
    wa jū-san-ji desu.
  • Jū-san-ji desu ka. Sore wa ichi-ji
    desu ne. Hai. Nan-ji ni Kyōto ni
    tsukimasu ka.
  ♦ Hai, Kyōto wa jū-go-ji han desu.
    Jū-go-ji han ni tsukimasu.
  • Jū-go-ji han desu ne. Hai, arigatō.
    *Ōsaka: 9 o'clock departure, 12 o'clock
    arrival; Kyōto: 1 o'clock departure, 3.30
    arrival*

5 • Sumimasen.
  ♦ Hai.
  • Ano, Tōkyō made ikura desu ka.
  ♦ Tōkyō desu ne. Ichi-mai desu ka.
  • Iie, san-mai desu.
  ♦ Hai, san-mai desu ne. Katamichi
    desu ka. Ōfuku desu ka.

  • Katamichi desu.
  ♦ Katamichi san-mai desu ne. Ēto …
    ¥3300 desu.
  • ¥3300 desu ne. Dōmo sumimasen.
  ♦ Iie.

  • Ano … sumimasen ga …
  ♦ Hai.
  • Kono jidō hanbaiki wa …
  ♦ Wakarimasen ka. Hai. Dochira
    made desu ka.
  • Yokohama made desu. Yokohama
    made ichi-mai.
  ♦ Ichi-mai desu ne. Hai. Katamichi
    desu ka. Ōfuku desu ka.
  • Ōfuku desu.
  ♦ Ōfuku ichi-mai desu ne. Hai,
    ¥14,800 desu.
  • ¥14,800 desu ne. Dōmo.
    *Tokyo – three tickets, single, ¥3,300;
    Yokohama – one ticket, return,
    ¥14,800*

6 • San-gatsu kokonoka no shinkansen
    desu ga.
  ♦ Hai. San-gatsu kokonoka desu ne.
  • Ēto … jū-ichi-ji san-jū-go-fun
    hatsu no Kōbe yuki, ni-mai
    kudasai.
  ♦ Hai, jū-ichi-ji san-jū-go-fun hatsu
    no Kōbe yuki desu ne.
  • Hai.
  ♦ Shitei-seki desu ka. Jiyū-seki desu
    ka.
  • A, shitei-seki o onegai shimasu.
  ♦ Katamichi desu ka. Ōfuku desu ka.
  • Katamichi o onegai shimasu. Ikura
    desu ka.
  ♦ Hai, Kōbe made, katamichi, ni-mai
    desu ne. ¥16,640 desu.
  • Sumimasen, mō ichido onegai
    shimasu.
  ♦ Hai, ¥16,640 desu.
  • Hai, dōzo. Nan-ji ni Kōbe ni
    tsukimasu ka.
  ♦ Jū-san-ji jū-go-fun ni tsukimasu.

- Jū-san-ji jū-go-fun desu ne.
  Arigatō.

a true; *b* false; *c* true; *d* true;
e false; *f* true

Page 82 Asking about public transport

2 • Sumimasen.
   ◆ Hai.
   • Kono densha wa Yokohama e ikimasu ka.
   ◆ Hai, ikimasu. Yokohama e ikimasu.
   • Dōmo arigatō.
   He wants to go to Yokohama. Yes, it does.

3 • Sumimasen, kono densha wa Hiroshima e ikimasu ka.
   ◆ Hiroshima desu ka. Iie ikimasen.
   • Sō desu ka. Hiroshima yuki wa nan-ban sen desu ka.
   ◆ Ni-ban sen desu. Asoko desu.

   • Sumimasen, kono basu wa Shibuya e ikimasu ka.
   ◆ Iie, Shibuya e ikimasen yo. Ano basu wa Shibuya e ikimasu yo.
   • Dono basu desu ka. Nan-ban desu ka.
   ◆ Jū-ichi-ban desu.
   • A, hai hai. Dōmo sumimasen.
   Train to Hiroshima, from platform 2. Bus to Shibuya, number 11.

Page 83 Taking a taxi

2 • **Sumitomo Biru made onegai shimasu.**
   ◆ Shinjuku desu ne.
   • Hai, Shinjuku no Sumitomo Biru, onegai shimasu.
   ◆ Hai, **wakarimashita** … Hai, Sumitomo Biru no mae desu ka.
   • **Koko de ii desu.**
   ◆ Hai, arigatō. ¥1350 desu ne … Hai, dōmo … ¥650 no o-tsuri desu.
   • **Ryōshūsho o onegai shimasu.**
   ◆ Hai, dōzo.

- Dōmo arigatō.
  ¥1350

3 • Sumimasen, Ginza no Guriin Hoteru made onegai shimasu.
   ◆ Ee? Doko desu ka. Sumimasen, mō ichido onegai shimasu.
   • Guriin Hoteru desu. Ginza ni arimasu.
   ◆ Guriin Hoteru desu ka.
   • Hai. Kore wa Guriin Hoteru no kādo desu. Dōzo. Jūsho wa koko desu.
   ◆ A, wakarimashita! Hai.
   He shows the driver the address on the hotel card.

4 *a* Green Hotel; *b* Ginza.

5 • Kono densha wa, Kōbe e ikimasu ka.
   ◆ Ōsaka yuki wa nan-ban sen desu ka.
   • Tōkyō eki made onegai shimasu.

Page 84 Put it all together

1 *a* 13.30 desu; *b* Iie, ōfuku desu;
c ¥2450 desu; *d* San-ban sen desu;
e Iie, ikimasu; *f* Iie, shitei-seki desu.

2 *a* jū-ichi-ji; *b* ni-ji han; *c* san-ji jū-go-fun; *d* hachi-ji ni-jup-pun; *e* roku-ji yon-jū-go-fun; *f* ku-ji jup-pun

3 *a* in a taxi; *b* on a station platform; *c* in a station booking office; *d* on a bus.

4 *a* ni; *b* e; *c* e; *d* wa; *e* ni; *f* wa

Page 85 Now you're talking!

1 • **Sumimasen, Hiroshima made ikura desu ka.**
   ◆ Hiroshima desu ne. Katamichi desu ka.
   • **Iie, ōfuku desu.**
   ◆ Hai. Nan-mai desu ka.
   • **Ichi-mai desu.**
   ◆ Hai, Hiroshima yuki, katamichi, ichi-mai desu ne. ¥14,350 desu.
   • **¥14,350 desu ne. Dōmo arigatō.**

2 • **Sumimasen, tsugi no Hiroshima yuki wa nan-ji desu ka.**
  ◆ Hai, 9.25 desu.
  • **Ku-ji ni-jū-go-fun desu ne. Nan-ji ni Hiroshima ni tsukimasu ka.**
  ◆ 13.05 ni tsukimasu.
  • **Nan-ban sen desu ka.**
  ◆ Hachi-ban sen desu.
  • **Arigatō.**

Page 86 Quiz
1 by bullet train; *2* unreserved seat; *3* departure; *4* no; *5* taxi driver; *6* a receipt; *7* wakarimashita; *8* platform 8.

Unit 10
Page 88 Saying what you like and don't like

2 • Itaria ryōri wa dō desu ka. Watashi wa piza ga suki desu ga … Ikeda-san wa?
  ◆ Watashi wa piza ga amari suki ja arimasen. Karē wa dō desu ka.
  • Karē wa chotto … Sushi wa dō desu ka. Chotto takai desu ga … Takahashi-san wa sushi ga suki desu ne.
  ◆ Hai, suki desu yo.
  They decide to have sushi.

3 • Nihon ryōri wa dō desu ka. Suki desu ka.
  ◆ Hai, dai-suki desu.
  • Sushi to sashimi wa?
  ◆ Hai, sushi mo sashimi mo suki desu.
  • Sō desu ka. Ja, soba wa?
  ◆ Soba wa kirai ja arimasen. Tōfu wa amari suki ja arimasen ga.
  • Sō desu ka. Tōfu wa suki ja arimasen ka. Yakitori wa?
  ◆ A, yakitori wa dai-suki desu yo. Yakitori to biiru!
  1 yakitori; *2, 3* sushi and sashimi; *4* soba; *5* tōfu.

Page 89 Asking about items on the menu

2 • Irasshaimase! Nan-mei sama desu ka.
  ◆ Roku-nin desu.
  • Roku-mei sama desu ne. Hai, dōzo, kochira e.

  • Irasshaimase! Nan-mei sama desu ka. San-mei sama desu ka.
  ◆ Hai, san-nin desu.
  • Dōzo, kochira e.
  6 people; 3 people

3 • Nani ni nasaimasu ka. Yakizakana wa dō desu ka.
  ◆ Yakizakana wa nan desu ka.
  • Sakana wa 'fish' desu ne. Yakizakana wa 'grilled fish' desu.
  ◆ Wakarimashita. Ja, tonkatsu wa Eigo de nan desu ka.
  • Eigo de 'pork cutlet' desu ne.
  ◆ Sō desu ka. Tonkatsu wa 'pork cutlet' desu ka.
  • Sashimi ga wakarimasu ne.
  ◆ Hai, sashimi wa 'raw fish' desu ne.
  • Hai, sō desu. Yakiniku wa?
  ◆ Niku wa 'meat' desu ka.
  • Hai, sō desu. Yakiniku wa 'grilled meat' desu ne. Ja, nani ni shimasu ka.
  ◆ Sō desu ne. Tonkatsu ni shimasu.
  • Tonkatsu desu ne.
  yakizakana = grilled fish; sashimi = raw fish; sakana = fish; niku = meat; tonkatsu = pork cutlet; yakiniku = grilled meat.
  She decides to order tonkatsu.

4 Sashimi wa Eigo de nan desu ka. Nihon ryōri ga dai suki desu. Sashimi wa amari suki ja arimasen.

Pages 90 & 91 Ordering a meal and paying compliments

2 • O-kimari desu ka.
  ◆ Kyō no ranchi setto wa nan desu ka.

- Hanbāgā setto to yakizakana setto ga gozaimasu.
- Ja, hanbāgā setto o kudasai.
- Watashi mo hanbāgā setto ni shimasu.
- Hai, raisu ni nasaimasu ka. Pan ni nasaimasu ka.
- Watashi wa pan desu.
- Raisu o onegai shimasu.
- Hai, hanbāgā setto o futatsu, raisu o hitotsu, pan o hitotsu desu ne. O-nomimono wa?
- Biiru o kudasai.
- Watashi wa kōra desu.
- Hai, biiru o ip-pon to kōra o hitotsu desu ne. Shōshō o-machi kudasai.
  Man: hanbāgā setto, pan, biiru
  Woman: hanbāgā setto, raisu, kōra

3
- Irasshaimase. O-kimari desu ka.
- Hai, yakitori o **kudasai**.
- Yakitori desu ne. Hai. **Nan-bon** desu ka.
- **Yon-hon** kudasai.
- **O-nomimono** wa?
- Biiru o **ni-hon** kudasai.

5
- Ii nioi desu ne. Nan desu ka.
- Kore desu ka. Shiitake desu.
- Shiitake desu ka. Oishi-sō desu ne. Ja, ni-hon kudasai.
- Shiitake o ni-hon desu ne. Hai.
- Arigatō.
- Dō desu ka.
- Mm, oishii!
Ikeda-san tries the shiitake.

6
- Sumimasen, o-kanjō o onegai shimasu.
- Hai, o-kanjō desu ne. ¥8500 desu.
- Hai. ¥8500.
- Dōmo arigatō gozaimashita.
- Gochisō sama deshita.
- Oishikatta desu ne. Yamada-san no yakiniku wa dō deshita ka.
- Totemo oishikatta desu. Yakiniku

wa dai-suki desu.
- Kono resutoran wa chotto takakatta desu ga, yokatta desu ne.
- Mm, sō desu ne.
  a are just leaving; b the bill; c meat; d ¥8500; e expensive

7 Yakitori wa oishi-sō desu ne! Ano resutoran wa takakatta desu ne!

Page 92 Put it all together

1 a It was delicious; b There are six people; c I don't like it; d Smells good, doesn't it! e Anything to drink? f I love it; g How is it?

2 a Sakana ga suki desu; b Nihon no biiru wa amari suki ja arimasen; c O-sake ga kirai desu; d Sashimi ga suki desu; e Itaria ryōri wa amari suki ja arimasen.

3 f; b; d; a; c; e

4 a Oishikatta desu; b Takakatta desu; c Atsukatta desu.

Page 93 Now you're talking!

1
- Nani ni shimasu ka.
- **Kore wa nan desu ka.**
- Tonkatsu desu.
- **Tonkatsu wa Eigo de nan desu ka.**
- 'Pork cutlet' desu. Niku wa suki desu ka.
- **Iie, amari suki ja arimasen.**
- Yakizakana wa dō desu ka.
- **Hai, yakizakana ni shimasu.**

2
- O-kimari desu ka.
- **Hanbāgā setto o onegai shimasu.**
- Hai. Pan ni nasaimasu ka. Raisu ni nasaimasu ka.
- **Pan o kudasai.**
- O-nomimono wa?
- **Biiru o kudasai.**
- Ip-pon desu ka.
- **San-bon kudasai.**
- Hai, shōshō o-machi kudasai.

3 ● Hanbāgā wa dō deshita ka.

 ◆ **Oishikatta desu.**

 ● Ii desu ne.

 ◆ **Sumimasen. O-kanjō o onegai shimasu.**

 ● Hai, ¥9450 desu.

 ◆ **Gochisō sama deshita.**

Page 94 Quiz

1 meat; *2* no; *3* Go-nin desu; *4* Nihon ryōri ga dai-suki desu; *5* sushi; *6* grilled; *7* no; *8* What you would like to drink; *9* It was expensive.

Chekkupointo 3

Pages 95-97

1 *b* Shinjuku Ōtani Hoteru made onegai shimasu.

2 ● Sumimasen, yoyaku o onegai shimasu.

 ◆ Hai, itsu deshō ka.

 ● Konban heya wa arimasu ka.

 ◆ Hai, gozaimasu. Shinguru deshō ka. Tsuin deshō ka.

 ● Tsuin o onegai shimasu.

 ◆ Hai, nan-paku desu ka.

 ● Suiyōbi made desu.

 ◆ Hai, 2-gatsu 26-nichi made desu. San-paku desu ne.

 ● Hai, san-paku desu.

 ◆ O-namae wa?

 ● Ikeda desu. Ikeda Haruo desu.
 a true; *b* true; *c* false; *d* true; *e* false

3 ● Hai, kochira ni o-namae to go-jūsho to denwa bangō o onegai shimasu. Hai, arigatō gozaimashita. O-heya wa 15-kai de gozaimasu. Dōzo, kochira e.
 a name; *b* address; *c* phone number; *d* 15th floor

4 ● Sumimasen, kore wa ikura desu ka.

 ◆ ¥3450 de gozaimasu.

 ● ¥3450 desu ka. Ja, mittsu kudasai.

 ◆ Hai, mittsu desu ne. Zenbu de ¥10,350 de gozaimasu.
 a ¥3450; *b* 3; *c* ¥10,350

5 *a* hoteru; *b* depāto; *c* eki; *d* kōban; *e* hoteru no bā; *f* yūbinkyoku

6 *a* O-shigoto wa?; *b* O-sumai wa Tōkyō desu ka; *c* Okusan wa o-ikutsu desu ka; *d* Okusan no o-namae wa?

7 *a* Itaria ryōri wa suki desu ka. Iie, amari suki ja arimasen; *b* Nan-mei sama desu ka. Go-nin desu; *c* Yakizakana wa Eigo de nan desu ka. 'Grilled fish' desu; *d* Nani ni nasaimasu ka. Tonkatsu o kudasai; *e* Yakiniku wa dō deshita ka. Oishikatta desu.

8 Across: *1* Kono hoteru ni pūru wa **arimasu** ka; *6* Nihon ryōri ga dai **suki** desu; *7* kōhii wa **ikaga** desu ka; *8* Pan ni shimasu ka. **Raisu** ni shimasu ka; *11* **Motto** chiisai desu. Chotto ōkii no wa arimasu; *13* **Ōfuku** desu ka. Katamichi desu ka; *15* Kono densha wa Tōkyō **yuki** desu ka; *18* Yakizakana wa totemo oishii desu ne; *19* Kyō wa **iya** na tenki desu na.

Down: *1* Dōmo **arigatō**; *2* Tanaka-san wa doko ni **imasu** ka; *3* Indo ryōri wa **amari** suki ja arimasen; *4* kōen wa eki no **ushiro** ni arimasu; *5* Nan-mei sama desu ka. San-**nin** desu; *9* Biiru ni-hon **to** o-sake ip-pon kudasai. *10* Hai, **o-kage** sama de, genki desu; *12* **Tsugi** no Nagoya yuki wa nan-ji desu ka; *14* Heya wa zenbu o-**furo** tsuki desu; *16* Sumimasen, **ima** nan-ji desu ka. *17* Kono resutoran **no** yakizakana wa oishii desu.

Written Japanese

Pages 98 & 99

1 kōhii (coffee); aisu kōhii (iced coffee); kokoa (cocoa); koka kōra (coca cola); miruku (milk); aisu kuriimu (ice cream); tōsuto (toast); kēki (cake); karē raisu (curry and rice); sutēki (steak)

2 isuraeru (Israel); itaria (Italy); iraku (Iraq); iran (Iran)

3 sutereo (stereo); eakon (air conditioner); kamera (camera); tōsutā (toaster); airon (iron); taoru (towel)

grammar

Grammar explains how a language works. When you're learning a new language it really helps to learn some basic rules, which are easier to follow if you understand these essential grammatical terms.

Nouns are the words for living beings, things, places and abstract concepts: *daughter, designer, Rachel, shark, hat, village, Tokyo, measles, freedom.*

Singular means one; **plural** means more than one.

Pronouns are words that can replace nouns. The most commonly used pronouns are **personal pronouns**, e.g. *you, she, him, we, it, they, them.*

Adjectives are words that describe nouns and pronouns: *good idea*; *strong red wine*; *she's tall*; *it was weird*.

Prepositions are words like *at, by, for, until* or *with* which introduce information regarding time, place, manner, purpose etc.

Particles are an important element of Japanese. They are small words that indicate the role of a word in a sentence – a concept that does not exist in English. Some particles also have similar roles to English prepositions.

Verbs relate to doing and being, and are easy to recognise in English because you can put *to* in front of them: *to live, to be, to speak, to explore, to think, to have, to need.*

The **subject** of a sentence is whoever or whatever is carrying out the action of the verb: *They have two children; Tomoko is going to Tokyo; Apples cost ¥500.*

The **object** of a sentence is at the receiving end of the verb. It can be **direct**: *They have two children*, or **indirect**: *I said 'hello' to the children*.

Japanese verbs have 'polite' and 'plain' forms depending on the level of formality required by the situation. In this book the polite form, suitable for everyday polite conversation, is used. The polite form ends in **-masu**.

hanashimasu *I/you speak* etc.
kakimasu *I/you write* etc.
kikimasu *I/you listen* etc.
machimasu *I/you wait* etc.
shinjimasu *I/you believe* etc.
akemasu *I/you open* etc.
agemasu *I/you give* etc.
nemasu *I/you sleep* etc.
wakarimasu *I/you understand* etc.
kimasu *I/you come* etc.
shimasu *I/you do/make* etc.

Verbs in Japanese behave differently from verbs in English. Unlike English, they stay the same regardless of who is carrying out the action, so **ikimasu** means *I go, you go, he/she goes* etc. It also translates *I'm going, you're going* etc., as well as *I/you/he/she will go*.

Mainichi 8.30 ni kaisha e ikimasu. *I go to work at 8.30 every day.*
Ashita kaisha e ikimasu. *I'm going/I will go to work tomorrow.*

When talking about the past, however, **-masu** changes to **-mashita**:

Kinō Kyōto e ikimashita. *Yesterday I went to Kyoto.*
Yoyaku shimashita. *I've made a reservation.*

Personal pronouns (*I, you, we*, etc.) are rarely used as long as the meaning can be understood from the context.
Amerika-jin desu. *I'm American.* (lit. *American am*)

When talking directly to someone, the person's name is generally used rather than the word for *you* or *your*.
Ikeda-san no kaisha wa dochira desu ka. *Where's your office, Mr Ikeda?* (lit. *Mr Ikeda's office where is?*)

In a dictionary, most verbs end in **-u** or **-ru** rather than **-masu**.

	-masu form	dictionary form
to go	**ikimasu**	**iku**
to drink	**nomimasu**	**nomu**
to work	**hatarakimasu**	**hataraku**
to buy	**kaimasu**	**kau**
to eat	**nomimasu**	**nomu**
to look at, see, watch	**mimasu**	**miru**

2 negatives

To make a sentence negative, simply change the ending of the verb:

-masu → -masen:

Wakarimasu ka. *Do you understand?*

Iie, wakarimasen. *No, I don't understand.*

-mashita → -masen deshita:

Wakarimashita ka. *Did you understand?*

Iie, wakarimasen deshita. *No, I didn't understand.*

	positive	negative
present/future	**-masu**	**-masen**
past	**-mashita**	**-masen deshita**

desu endings

Desu *I am, you are* etc. is not technically a verb in Japanese but it serves a similar function.

	positive	negative
present/future	**desu**	**ja arimasen***
past	**deshita**	**ja arimasen deshita**

*You will also come across the more formal **dewa arimasen**.

Nihon-jin desu ka. *Are you Japanese?*

Iie, Nihon-jin ja arimasen. *No, I'm not Japanese.*

G4 to be

There are three ways of saying *am/is/are*:
Arimasu is used for something inanimate (objects and events). **Imasu** is used for something animate (people, animals and birds).

Hoteru ni pūru ga <u>arimasu</u>. *<u>There's</u> a pool in the hotel.*
Kaisha wa Yokohama ni <u>arimasu</u>. *My office <u>is</u> in Yokohama.*

Kōen ni hito ga takusan <u>imasu</u>. *<u>There are</u> a lot of people in the park.*
Yamada-san wa doko ni <u>imasu</u> ka. *Where <u>is</u> Mr Yamada?*

Desu is used to talk about states or attributes.
Kyō wa 3-gatsu 25-nichi <u>desu</u>. *Today <u>is</u> March 25th.*
Yamada-san wa enjinia <u>desu</u>. *Mr Yamada <u>is</u> an engineer.*

G5 word order

The main rule to remember about Japanese word order is that
the verb (and **desu**) come at the end of the sentence:
John-san wa sushi o <u>tabemasu</u>. *John <u>eats</u> sushi.* (lit. *John sushi <u>eats</u>*.)

Other than this, the word order is flexible, but the subject or topic
usually comes first and expressions of time usually come before
expressions of place:
John-san wa <u>kinyōbi</u> ni Tōkyō ni ikimasu.
John is going to Tokyo <u>on Friday</u>.
(lit. *John on Friday to Tokyo is going*.)

G6 particles

Words within the sentence are accompanied by markers (known as
particles) to show the role they play in the sentence and these must
come directly after the word they're marking.
John-san <u>wa</u> sushi <u>o</u> tabemasu. *John (topic) eats sushi (object).*

Each particle often has several functions depending on the combination
of words, context or sentence pattern. The explanations given here
relate to their usage within this book and you will learn other functions
as your Japanese progresses.

wa, ga and o

Japanese sentences often start with a noun followed by **wa**. This is called the topic marker and is used to indicate what the rest of the sentence is about. It can be thought of as meaning '*as for*' or '*regarding*'.

Watashi <u>wa</u> Yamada desu. *I am Yamada* (lit. *As for me, Yamada am.*)
John-san <u>wa</u> Igirisu-jin desu. *John is British.* (lit. *As for John, British is.*)

Ga is the grammatical marker for the subject of the verb:
Hoteru ni <u>kissaten</u> ga arimasu. *There's a coffee shop in the hotel.* (lit. *In the hotel <u>coffee shop</u> is.*)

One of the main difficulties for a learner of Japanese is that the subject of the verb can often be the topic of the sentence. Deciding between **wa** and **ga** is not simple and relies heavily on the context in which the sentence appears, so the best way for beginners to learn when to use **ga** instead of **wa**, is to learn it within set phrases. The following are the most common and useful sentences in which **ga** is used:

1. ... **ga wakarimasu** *understand*
Eigo ga wakarimasu ka. *Do you understand English?* (lit. *English is understandable?*)

2. ... **ga irimasu** *need*
Biza ga irimasu. *I need a visa.* (lit. *Visa is necessary.*)

3. ... **ga suki desu** *like*
Kōhii ga sukidesu. *I like coffee.* (lit. *Coffee is likeable.*)

4. ... **ga arimasu/imasu** *there is/there are*
Denwa ga arimasu. *There is a telephone.*
Hito ga takusan imasu. *There are a lot of people.*

O shows the object of the verb:
Sono <u>kamera o</u> misete kudasai.   *Please show me that <u>camera</u>.*
<u>Kōhii o</u> onegai shimasu.   *I'd like a <u>coffee</u>, please.*

wa versus **ga**

If someone asks you a question using **wa**, you are likely to need **wa** in the answer:

Kaisha wa doko desu ka./Kaisha wa doko ni arimasu ka. *Where is your office?*

Kaisha wa Rondon ni arimasu. *My office is in London.*

Another useful way of choosing between **wa** and **ga** is to think about which piece of information in the sentence is the most important.

A **wa** B / A **ga** B: if the information in B is important, use **wa** and if the information in A is important, use **ga**.

For example:

John-san wa sushi o tabemasu.

   A   B

John is eating sushi. (In answer to *What is John eating?*)

John-san ga sushi o tabemasu.

  A   B

John is eating sushi. (In answer to *Who is eating sushi?*)

Yamada-san wa asoko ni imasu.

  A   B

Mr Yamada is over there. (in answer to *Where is Mr Yamada?*)

Yamada-san ga asoko ni imasu.

  A   B

Mr Yamada is over there. (in answer to *Who is over there?*)

So '**ga**' is often used when introducing a new subject into the conversation.

7 ni, de and e

Some particles are similar to English prepositions, words such as *in*, *at*, *on*, but, unlike in English, they always follow the word or words they mark:

Yamada-san wa / 8.30 ni / densha de / kaisha e / ikimasu.
Mr Yamada goes to work by train at 8.30. (lit. *As for Mr Yamada / at 8.30 / by train / to the office / he goes.*)

ni

ni is generally used after expressions of time to mean *at*, *on* or *in*:

Rokuji ni okimasu. *I get up at 6am.*
Kayōbi ni kaisha e ikimasen. *I'm not going to work on Tuesday.*

With the verb 'to be' **ni** also means *in* or *at* a place:

Tanaka-san wa bā ni imasu. *Mr Tanaka is in the bar.*

With verbs of motion **ni** means *to* or *toward*:

Yamada-san wa Yokohama ni ikimasu. *Mr Yamada is going to Yokohama.*

de

De indicates a location in which action takes place:

Resutoran de Sushi o tabemashita. *I ate sushi at a restaurant.*
and after modes of transport it means *by*:

Chikatetsu de kaisha e ikimasu. *I go to the office by underground.*

e

Like **ni**, the particle **e** is used to show motion *to* or *toward* a place:

Kono densha wa Tōkyō e ikimasu ka? *Does this train go to Tokyo?*

no

Possession or belonging is shown by adding the particle **no** to the person who owns the object, rather like the English *'s*, e.g. **Tanaka-san no uchi** *Mr Tanaka's house*; **tsuma no kuruma** *my wife's car*; **kaisha no denwa bangō** *the company's phone number*.

It is also used in a much wider sense to join two nouns together where the first helps to describe the second.

Toyota no Takeda-san *Mr Takeda of Toyota* (lit. *Toyota's Mr Takeda*)
ashita no 2.30 *2.30 tomorrow* (lit. *tomorrow's 2.30*)

When two nouns are put together to make a compound noun, these are usually joined by **no**:

eigo no sensei *English teacher*
Nihongo no kurasu *Japanese class*

asking questions

Questions are formed by adding the particle **ka** to the end of the sentence. No question mark is needed.

John-san wa sushi o tabemasu <u>ka</u>. *Does John eat sushi?*

If you want to ask an 'either/or' question, just ask two separate questions:

Raisu desu ka. Pan desu ka. *Would you like rice or bread?*

A very simple way of asking a question when enquiring about the existence of something is to use the noun followed by the particle **wa**, with your voice rising at the end of the sentence:

Shawā wa? *Is there/How about a shower?*
O-shigoto wa? *What do you do?* (lit. *Your job?*)
These need a question mark.

When using a question word such as *what* **nan/nani**, *when* **itsu** and *where* **doko**, these go in the same place as the answer would be in the sentence:

Ano biru wa <u>nan</u> desu ka. *What is that building?* (lit. *As for that building, what is?*)
Ano biru wa <u>ginkō</u> desu. *That building is a bank.*

> If you're listening to or reading Japanese, it helps if you pay attention to the end of the sentence as this is where much of the important information is: you can tell whether a statement is positive or negative, whether it's talking about the past or the present and whether or not it is a question. If you hear **ka** at the end of the sentence, you know that you need to be ready with an answer.

G10 **nouns**

Japanese nouns don't have plural forms, so **kutsu** can mean *shoe* or *shoes*. The context will normally make it clear whether the noun is singular or plural.

There are no words for *the/a/an* or *some/any* so the sentence **<u>Ringo</u> ga arimasu** can mean *I have <u>an apple</u>* or *I have <u>some apples</u>* (as well as *there is an apple/there are some apples*).

1 counters

Japanese uses numbers and 'counters' to count objects. These counters are similar to phrases in English like *a glass of*, *a sheet of* and they change according to the shape of the object. For example, long thin objects such as pens and bottles are counted with the number + **-hon**, **-pon**, or **-bon**, flat objects such as stamps, postcards and pizzas are counted with **-mai** and people are counted with **-nin** (except for 1 and 2 which are **hitori** and **futari**). Counters are attached to the number (e.g. **san-bon**, **san-mai**) and come after the noun.

biiru ni-hon *two beers*
hagaki go-mai *five postcards*
tomodachi san-nin *three friends*

There is an all-purpose system of numbers for counting up to ten which can be used when no other counter is appropriate: **hitotsu** (one object), **futatsu**, **mittsu, yottsu, itsutsu, muttsu, nanatsu, yattsu, kokonotsu, tō**.
hanbāgā futatsu *two hamburgers*

> If you're not sure which counting system to use, you can always resort to the all-purpose system (**hitotsu**, **futatsu**, etc.). You will still be understood. However, don't use this to count people as it is considered offensive.

2 adjectives

Japanese adjectives fall into two categories, '**-i** adjectives' and '**-na** adjectives'.

-i adjectives
Most Japanese adjectives fall into this category. They end in **-ai**, **-oi**, **-ii** or **-ui**:
chiisai *small*, **omoshiroi** *interesting*, **tanoshii** *enjoyable*, **warui** *bad*

These adjectives can behave like verbs and so they have different forms for the negative and past tense.

tense	ending	example
present and future	**-i**	**chiisai (desu)** *it's small*
present and future negative	**-kunai**	**chiisakunai (desu)** *it isn't small*
past	**-katta**	**chiisakatta (desu)** *it was small*
past negative	**-kunakatta**	**chiisakunakatta (desu)** *it wasn't small*

ii *good* is the only irregular adjective:
ii desu *it's good*
yokunai desu *it isn't good*
yokatta desu *it was good*
yokunakatta desu *it wasn't good*

-na adjectives
All other adjectives fall into this category. They're called **-na** adjectives because when they're used before a noun, they end in **-na**:
Hayashi-san wa <u>shinsetsu</u> desu. *Mr Hayashi is <u>kind</u>.*
Hayashi-san wa <u>shinsetsuna</u> hito desu. *Mr Hayashi is a <u>kind</u> person.*

When they're used in the past tense or the negative, they use the appropriate form of **desu**:
Hayashi-san wa shinsetsu <u>deshita</u>. *Mr Hayashi <u>was</u> kind.*
Hayashi-san wa shinsetsu <u>ja arimasen deshita</u>. *Mr Hayashi <u>wasn't</u> kind.*

In Japanese, the expression *to like* uses an **-na** adjective **suki(na)** meaning *favourite/likeable*:
Tenisu ga suki desu. *I like tennis.* (lit. *Tennis is likeable.*)

common i-adjectives

atarashii	*new*	**furui**	*old*
atsui	*hot*	**samui**	*cold* (weather)
oishii	*delicious*	**mazui**	*bad tasting*
okii	*big*	**chiisai**	*small*
omoshiroi	*interesting, funny*	**tsumaranai**	*boring*
chikai	*near*	**toi**	*far*

nagai	long	mijikai	short
muzukashii	difficult	yasashii	easy
takai	tall, expensive	yasui	cheap

common na-adjectives

ijiwaruna	mean	shinsetsuna	kind
shizukana	quiet	nigiyakana	lively
kikenna	dangerous	anzenna	safe
benrina	convenient	fubenna	inconvenient
kireina	pretty	genkina	healthy, well
teineina	polite	shojikina	honest

Adjectives can be made into nouns by adding **no**:

ōkii *big*   **ōkii no** *big one(s)*
akai *red*   **akai no** *red one(s)*

politeness levels

Different styles of speech are used in Japanese to show the degree of formality and politeness. This depends on the relationship between the speaker and the listener (teacher – student, employee – boss, sales assistant – customer, older person – younger person) and the degree of respect which needs to be shown. It involves the use of different verbs and 'honorific' terms when referring to others, and 'humble' terms when referring to oneself.

All verbs have a plain and polite form (see verbs) and a few have super-polite forms, used to talk to customers in shops, hotels and restaurants:
Waitress: **Nani ni <u>nasaimasu</u> ka.** *What will you <u>have</u>?*
Customer: **Piza ni <u>shimasu</u>.** *I'll <u>have</u> the pizza.*

Customer: **Ikura <u>desu</u> ka.** *How much <u>is it</u>?*
Sales assistant: **¥2500 <u>de gozaimasu</u>.** *<u>It's</u> ¥2500.*

O- is added to the beginning of some words as a mark of respect to the person you're speaking to, for example when asking someone's name (**O-namae wa?**) or what they do for a living (**O-shigoto wa?**).

In some cases, completely different words may be used.

kanai/tsuma *my wife*   **okusan** *your wife*
jūsho *address, my address*   **go-jūsho** *your address*

There are polite ways of asking for and receiving things, equivalent to the English *please* and *thank you*. **O kudasai** is used when asking for an object and **onegai shimasu** when asking someone to do something for you:

Chiizu sando o kudasai. (*I'd like*) *a cheese sandwich please.*
O-kanjō o onegai shimasu. (*Could you bring*) *the bill please.*

Arigatō gosaimasu means *thank you* and when thanking someone for something which has already been done or completed it is used in the past tense: **arigatō gosaimashita**. **Dōmo** is a more informal way of saying *thanks*.

G14 demonstratives

In the absence of words for *the* and *a* Japanese makes more use of words such as *this*, *that*, *these* and *those*. A distinction is made to show whether something is near the speaker (**kore, kono**), near the listener (**sore, sono**) or away from both the speaker and the listener (**are, ano**).

dore	kore	sore	are
which (one/s)?	*this/these (one/s)*	*that/those (one/s)*	*that/those (one/s) over there*
dono	**kono**	**sono**	**ano**
which (+ noun)?	*this/these (+ noun)*	*that/those (+ noun)*	*that/those (+ noun) over there*
doko*	**koko**	**soko**	**asoko**
where?	*here*	*there*	*over there*

[***dochira** is a polite form of *where*.]

Kono kamera wa takai desu. *This camera is expensive.*
Sono beruto o misete kudasai. *Please could I see that belt?*
Ano biru desu. *It's that building over there.*
Kore wa hoteru desu ka. *Is this a hotel?*

wordpower

In Japanese there are a large number of words which have come from other languages. For example, *taxi* in Japanese is **takushii**, *bread* is **pan** (from the Portuguese **pão**) and *part-time job* is **arubaito**, which comes from the German word for *work*, **arbeit**.

The pronunciation of these words has been assimilated into the Japanese system, so some may take a little more working out than others:

technology

intānetto *internet*

tekisuto *text message*

ii-mēru *email*

uebusaito *website*

conpyūtā *computer*

memorii kādo *memory card*

taburetto *tablet*

travel

furaito *flight*

pasupōto *passport*

basu *bus*

apāto *apartment*

bijinesu hoteru *business hotel*

yūsu hosuteru *youth hostel*

shinguru rūmu *single room*

daburu rūmu *double room*

tsuin rūmu *twin room*

famirii rūmu *family room*

bebii beddo *cot*

chekku auto *check-out*

sport

fittonesu sentā *fitness centre*

pūru *swimming pool*

tenisukōto *tennis court*

sakkā *football, soccer*

basukettobōru *basketball*

gorufu *golf*

sukii *skiing*

sāfin *surfing*

sunō bōdo *snowboarding*

clothes

jaketto *jacket*

T shatsu *t-shirt*

beruto *belt*

wanpiisu *dress*

pantsu *(women's) trousers*

nekutai *tie*

sūtsu *suit*

sētah *sweater*

jiinzu *jeans*

eating and drinking

resutoran *restaurant*

bā *bar*

menyū *menu*

mein cōsu *main course*

naifu *knife*

fōku *fork*

supūn *spoon*

napukin *napkin*

biiru *beer*

shanpen *champagne*

jintonikku *gin and tonic*

furūtsu jūsu *fruit juice*

māmarēdo *marmalade*

tōsuto *toast*

hotto doggu *hotdog*

ramu *lamb*

sūpu *soup*

painappuru *pineapple*

orenji *orange*

remon *lemon*

meron *melon*

karifurawā *cauliflower*

bejitarian *vegetarian*

nattsu *nuts*

arerugii *allergic*

professions

direkutā *director*

anaunsā *announcer*

bijinesuman *businessman*

jānarisuto *journalist*

general

handobaggu *handbag*

buriifukeisu *briefcase*

garēji *garage*

hankachi *handkerchief*

herikoputā *helicopter*

intabyū *interview*

magajin *magazine*

kontakuto renzu *contact lens*

esukarētā *escalator*

yōroppa *Europe*

Some words of foreign origin are shortened in Japanese. For example, *PC* (*personal computer*) is **paso-kon** and *convenience store* is **conbini**; *smart phone* is **sumaho**.

top ten essentials

1 Talking about people:
   (Watashi wa) Igirisu-jin desu. *I am British.*
   (Watashi wa) gakusei ja arimasen. *I am not a student.*
   (Anata wa) Nihon-jin desu ka. *Are you Japanese?*

2 Talking about what's available:
   Pūru ga arimasu. *There's a pool.*
   O-mise ga arimasu. *There are shops.*
   Bā ga arimasu ka. *Is there a bar?*

3 Talking about having:
   Jitensha ga arimasu. *I've got a bike.*
   Chizu ga arimasu ka. *Do you have the map?*
   Shitsumon ga arimasu. *We have some questions.*

4 Asking what things are:
   Kore wa nan desu ka. *What is this?*
   ... wa nihongo de nan desu ka. *How do you say/What is ...
   in Japanese?*

5 Asking where things are:
   Iriguchi/deguchi wa doko desu ka. *Where is the entrance/exit?*
   Apāto wa doko desu ka. *Where is/are the apartment(s)?*

6 Saying what you like:
   Nihon ga suki desu. *I like Japan.*
   Ryoko ga suki desu. *I like travelling.*

7 Saying or asking if you need something:
   Jisho ga irimasu. *I need a dictionary.*
   Pasupoto ga irimasu ka. *Do I need a passport?*

8 Asking for something:
   Kohii o kudasai. *Please could I have a coffee.*
   Eigo no menyū o kudasai. *An English menu, please.*

9 Asking somebody to do something:
   Mō ichido onegai shimasu. *Please could you repeat it?*
   (Motto) yukkuri onegai shimasu. *(More) slowly please...*
   ... Nihongo ga sukoshi wakarimasu. *I understand a little Japanese.*

10 Imposing and apologising:
   Sumimasen. *Sorry.* (informal)/*Excuse me.*
   Mōshiwake arimasen. *I am sorry.* (polite – lit. *There is no excuse.*)

Japanese–English glossary

This glossary contains only those words and phrases, and their meanings, as they occur in **Talk Japanese**.

A

airon iron
Airurando Ireland
aisu kōhii ice coffee
aisu kuriimu ice cream
aite imasu to be open
amari not really, not very (with negative)
Amerika America, USA
ano that … over there
apāto apartment, flat
appuru pai apple pie
appuru jūsu apple juice
are that (one)/those (ones) … over there
arigatō thank you;
arigatō gozaimasu thank you very much
arimasu there is/are, to be, have (used with objects)
ashita tomorrow
asoko over there
atarashii new
atsui hot (weather);
atsukatta was hot

B

bā bar
banana banana
-ban sen platform
bangō number
basu bus
(o-)bentō boxed lunch
beruto belt
biiru beer
biru building
Burajiru Brazil

C

(o-)cha green tea
chigaimasu it isn't correct
chiisai small
chiizu cheese
chiizukēki cheesecake
chikaku nearby
chokorēto chocolate
chōshoku breakfast
chotto rather, a little

D

daburu double room
dai-kirai dislike very much
dai-suki like very much
de gozaimasu is, are (polite form of **desu**)
deguchi exit
densha train
denwa phone
denwa bangō phone number
depāto department store
deshita was, were
deshō is, are, will be (polite form of **desu**)
desu I am, you are, he/she/it is, we/you/they are
dewa arimasen isn't/aren't
dō how about …?
dochira where, in what direction? (polite)
doko where?
dōmo thanks
dono which?
dorai kuriiningu dry cleaning
dore which one(s)
doyōbi Saturday
dōzo here you are, please have this
dōzo yoroshiku pleased to meet you

E

e to, towards
eakon air conditioning
ee yes
Eigo English language
Eigo de in English
eki train station
en yen
enjinia engineer
erebētā lift

F

fakkusu fax
-fun/-pun minute
Furansu France
furo bath
furonto front desk, reception
futari (two people)
futatsu two (when counting objects)
futon Japanese bedding
futsuka second (of the month)

G

ga (indicates previous word is subject of sentence)
gakusei student
gārufurendo girlfriend
-gatsu (counter for names of months)
genki well, healthy

(o-)genki desu ka Are you well?

getsuyōbi Monday

ginkō bank

ginkōin bank worker

go five

gochisō sama deshita (set phrase said after eating)

go-gatsu May

go-shōkai shimasu let me introduce you

go-shujin (your) husband

gozaimasu have, exist (polite form of **arimasu**)

guriin green

H

hachi eight

hachi-gatsu August

hagaki postcard

hai yes

hajimemashite how do you do?

-haku/-paku (counter for overnight stays)

hamu ham

han half

hanbāgā hamburger

hatachi 20 years old

hatsu departure

hatsuka twentieth (of the month)

heya room

hidari left (direction)

hito person, people

hitori one person

hitotsu one (when counting objects)

-hon (counter for long, thin objects)

hoteru hotel

hyaku hundred

chi one

chido once

chi-gatsu January

Igirisu England, Britain

ii good, fine, well

iie (in response to **arigatō**) you're welcome

iie no

ikaga how about?

ikimasu go

ikura how much?

(o-)ikutsu how old?

ima now

imasu there is/are, to be (used with living things)

Indo India

ip-paku one overnight stay

Iraku Iraq

Iran Iran

irasshaimase! welcome!

iriguchi entrance

isha doctor

Isuraeru Israel

itadakimasu (set phrase said before eating)

Itaria Italy

itsu when?

itsuka fifth (of the month)

itsutsu five (when counting objects)

iya-na horrible

izakaya bar, drinking place

J

ja arimasen isn't, aren't

ja well then

-ji o'clock

jidō hanbaiki vending machine

-jin person from (name of country)

jiyū-seki unreserved seat

jū ten

jū-gatsu October

jū-ichi gatsu November

jū-ni gatsu December

jū-yokka fourteenth (of the month)

(go)jūsho address

jūsu juice

K

ka (word showing that the sentence is a question)

kādo card

-kai counter for floors of a building

kaisha company

kaishain office worker

kamera camera

Kanada Canada

kanai (my) wife

kankō annaijo tourist information office

(o-)kanjō bill

kanpai! Cheers!

kara from

karē curry;

karē raisu curry and rice

Karifurunia California

katamichi one-way

kayōbi Tuesday

kēki cake

kekkō enough, fine;

kekkō desu I've had enough!

kin-en no smoking

kinyōbi Friday

kiosuku kiosk

kirai dislike

kiromētoru kilometre

kissaten coffee shop

kitte stamp

kōban police box

kōcha (black) tea

kochira this, this person, this way (polite)

kochira e this way, please

kōen park

kōhii coffee

koko here

kokoa cocoa

kokonoka ninth (of the month)

kōkūbin air mail;

kōkūbin de by air mail

konban this evening

konbanwa good evening

konnichiwa hello, good afternoon
kono this/these
kōra cola
kore this (one)/these (ones)
kudasai could I have …?
(o-)kuni country
kuriimu cream
kutsu shoes
kyō today
kyū/ku nine
kū-gatsu September

M

made towards, as far as
mae in front of
-mai (counter for flat objects)
mainichi every day
man ten thousand
Manchesutā Manchester
Maruta Malta
massugu straight ahead;
massugu itte go straight ahead, and …
matsuri festival
meishi business card
Mekishiko Mexico
meron melon
migi right (direction)
mikka third (of the month)
mikkusu sando mixed sandwich
miruku milk;
miruku tii milk tea
misete kudasai please show me
mittsu three (when counting objects)
mō again;
mō ichido once again
mo too, also
mokuyōbi Thursday
mōningu setto breakfast set menu
moshi moshi hello (on the phone)

motto more;
motto yukkuri more slowly
muika sixth (of the month)
mukai opposite
mushiatsui hot and humid

N

nai-sen bangō phone extension number
naka in, inside
(o-)namae name
nan-ban sen which platform?
nan-ban what number?
nan-bon how many? (counter for long, thin objects)
nan-gatsu which month?
nan-ji what time?
nan-mai how many (flat objects)?
nan-mei sama how many people? (formal)
nan-paku how many nights' stay?
nana seven
nani/nan what?
nanoka seventh (of the month)
nanyōbi what day?
nasaimasu to have, order (polite)
ne isn't it? aren't they? etc.
Nepāru Nepal
ni in, at, two
ni-gatsu February
ni-jū-yokka twenty-fourth (of the month)
ni-shoku two meals
-nichi counter for dates
nichiyōbi Sunday
Nihon Japan; **Nihon de wa** in Japan
Nihongo Japanese language
niku meat
-nin (counter for people)

nioi smell
no of (shows possession)
nomimono a drink

O

o (this word indicates the object of a verb)
ōfuku return ticket
ohayō morning!;
ohayō gozaimasu good morning
oishi-sō looks delicious
oishii delicious
oishikatta was delicious
o-kage sama de thank you for asking
ōkii big
o-kimari desu ka Have you decided? (formal)
okusan (your) wife
omedetō congratulations
onegai shimasu please (do me this favour)
onna woman
Oranda Holland
orenji jūsu orange juice
oshibori moist handtowel
Ōsutoraria Australia
otoko man
oyasumi nasai goodnight

P

painappuru pineapple
pan bread
Pari Paris
piza pizza
poteto chippu crisps
pūru pool

R

raisu rice with a western-style meal
ranchi lunch; **ranchi setto** lunch set menu
raunji lounge
rei nought
remon jūsu lemon squash
remon tii lemon tea

resutoran restaurant
ringo apple
robii lobby
roku six
roku-gatsu June
Rondon London
ryokan Japanese-style inn
ryōri cooking, cuisine
ryōshūsho receipt

S

-sai years old
saizu size
sakana fish
sake rice wine
sakura cherry blossom, cherry tree
samui cold
san three
san-gatsu March
sando(itchi) sandwich
sarariiman salaried worker
sashimi raw fish
-san Mr, Mrs, Ms
-satsu (counter for publications)
sayōnara goodbye
sen thousand
sensei teacher
setto set meal
shawā shower
shi four
shichi seven
shi-gatsu April
shibaraku desu ne It's been a long time, hasn't it!
shichi-gatsu July
shigoto job
shiitake shiitake mushrooms
(ni)shimasu to have, order
shinbun newspaper
shingō traffic lights
shinguru single room
shinkansen bullet train
shitei-seki reserved seat
shitsurei desu ga excuse me, but …

shitsurei shimasu please excuse me, goodbye
shōkai introduction (of people)
shokuji meal
shōshō o-machi kudasai please wait a moment (formal)
shufu housewife
shujin (my) husband
sō desu that's right;
sō desu ka really?
soba buckwheat noodles
soko there
sono that
sore kara and also, then
sore that (one)/those (ones)
Suēden Sweden
suiyōbi Wednesday
suki like
Sukottorando Scotland
sukoshi a little, small amount
(o-)sumai your home (polite)
sumimasen excuse me
supōtsu senta sports centre
sushi bite-sized delicacies served on vinagered rice
sutēki steak
sutereo stereo

T

Tai Thailand
takai expensive;
takakatta was expensive
takusan many, a lot of
takushii taxi
taoru towel
tatami straw mat flooring
tegami letter
tenki weather
(o-)tearai washroom, toilet
terebi television

to and
tōfu tofu
tōka tenth (of the month)
tokei watch
tomato tomato
(o-)tomodachi friend
tonari next to
tonkatsu pork cutlet
toire toilet
toshokan library
tōsutā toaster
tōsuto toast
tsugi no next, following
tsuin twin room
tsuitachi first (of the month)
tsuki including
tsukimasu arrive
(o-)tsuri change (money)
(o-)tsutome your place of work

U

uchi house, home
Uēruzu Wales
ushiro behind

W

wa (word showing the topic of sentence)
wain wine
wakai young
wakarimasen I don't know, I don't understand;
wakarimashita I understand, understood
wakarimasu ka Do you understand?
washitsu Japanese-style room
watashi I, me;
watashi no my

Y

yakiniku grilled meat
yakitori barbecued chicken
yakitori-ya yakitori shop
yakizakana grilled fish
yasui cheap

yasumi day off, holiday, closed

yo (emphasizes the preceeding words)

yōka eighth (of the month)

yokatta was good

yokka fourth (of the month)

yon four

yōshitsu Western-style room

yottsu four (when counting objects)

yoyaku shimashita made a reservation

yūbinkyoku post office

yuki bound for, going to

yukkuri slowly

yūshoku evening meal

Z

zenbu all; **zenbu de** altogether

zero zero

English–Japanese glossary

A

address (go)jūsho
again mō, mōichido
air conditioning eakon
air mail kōkūbin; by air mail kōkūbin de
all zenbu
altogether zenbu de
am not ja arimasen (neg of desu); imasen
America Amerika
and to
apartment apāto
apple ringo; apple juice appuru jūsu; apple pie appuru pai
April shi-gatsu
aren't ja arimasen (neg of desu); arimasen; imasen; aren't they? ne
arrive tsukimasu
as far as made
at ni
August hachi-gatsu
Australia Ōsutoraria

B

banana banana
bank ginkō; bank worker ginkōin
bar bā; (Japanese-style) izakaya
barbecued chicken yakitori
bath furo
to be desu; (used with objects) arimasu; (used with living things) imasu
beer biiru
behind ushiro
belt beruto
big ōkii
bill (o-)kanjō
boxed lunch (o-)bentō
Brazil Burajiru
bread pan

breakfast chōshoku, asagohan; breakfast set menu mōningu setto
Britain Igirisu
buckwheat noodles soba
building biru
bullet train shinkansen
bus basu
business: business card meishi; business man sarariiman

C

cake kēki
California Kariforunia
camera kamera
Canada Kanada
card kādo
change (money) (o-)tsuri
cheap yasui
Cheers! kanpai!
cheese chiizu
cheesecake chiizukēki
cherry blossom sakura
cherry tree sakura
chocolate chokorēto
closed yasumi
cocoa kokoa
coffee kōhii; coffee shop kissaten
cola kōra
cold (weather) samui; (cold to the touch) tsumetai
company kaisha
congratulations omedetō
cooking, cuisine ryōri
correct: it isn't correct chigaimasu
country (o-)kuni
cream kuriimu
crisps poteto chippu
curry karē; curry and rice karē raisu
day off yasumi

D

December jū-ni gatsu
decide: Have you decided? (formal) O-kimari desu ka
delicious oishii; was delicious oishikatta; looks delicious oishi-sō
department store depāto
departure hatsu
dislike kirai; dislike very much dai-kirai
doctor isha
double room daburu
a drink nomimono
dry cleaning dorai kuriiningu

E

eight hachi
eighth (of the month) yōka
engineer enjinia
England Igirisu
English (language) Eigo; in English Eigo de
enough kekkō; I've had enough! kekkō desu!
entrance iriguchi
evening: this evening konban
evening meal yūshoku, bangohan
every day mainichi
excuse me sumimasen; excuse me, but … shitsurei desu ga; please excuse me, goodbye shitsurei shimasu
exit deguchi
expensive takai; was expensive takakatta

F

fax fakkusu
February ni-gatsu
festival matsuri
fifth (of the month) itsuka

fine **ii**
first (of the month) **tsuitachi**
fish **sakana**
five **go**; (when counting objects) **itsutsu**
following (next) **tsugi no**
four **yon**; (when counting objects) **yottsu**
fourteenth (of the month) **jū-yokka**
fourth (of the month) **yokka**
France **Furansu**
Friday **kinyōbi**
friend **(o-)tomodachi**
from **kara**

G

girlfriend **gārufurendo**
go **ikimasu**; going to, bound for **yuki**
go straight ahead, and … **massugu itte**
good **ii**; was good **yokatta**
good afternoon **konnichiwa**
good evening **konbanwa**
good morning **ohayō gozaimasu**
goodbye **sayōnara, shitsurei shimasu**
goodnight **oyasumi nasai**
green **guriin, midori**
green tea **(o-)cha**
grilled fish **yakizakana**
grilled meat **yakiniku**

H

half **han**
ham **hamu**
hamburger **hanbāgā**
hand towel (wipe) **oshibori**
to have **imasu; arimasu**; (order) **(ni)shimasu**; could I have …? … **kudasai**
hello **konnichiwa**; (on the phone) **moshi moshi**
here **koko**

here you are **dōzo**
holiday **yasumi**
Holland **Oranda**
home **uchi**; your home (polite) **(o-)sumai**
horrible **iya-na**
hot (weather) **atsui**; was hot **atsukatta**; hot and humid **mushiatsui**
hotel **hoteru**
house **uchi, ie**; your house (polite) **(o-)sumai**
housewife **shufu**
how about …? **dō, ikaga**
how do you do? **hajimemashite**
how many? (flat objects) **nan-mai**; (long, thin objects) **nan-bon**; how many nights' stay? **nan-paku**; how many people? (formal) **nan-mei sama**
how much? **ikura**
how old? **(o-)ikutsu**
hundred **hyaku**
(my) husband **shujin, otto**; (your) husband **go-shujin**

I

I **watashi**
iced coffee **aisu kōhii**
ice cream **aisu kuriimu**
in front of **mae**
in **ni**; (inside) **naka**
including **tsuki, komi**
India **Indo**
inn (Japanese-style) **ryokan**
introduce: let me introduce you **go-shōkai shimasu**
introduction (of people) **shōkai**
Iran **Iran**
Iraq **Iraku**
Ireland **Airurando**
iron **airon**
isn't **ja arimasen** (neg of **desu**); **arimasen; imasen**;

isn't it? **ne**
Israel **Isuraeru**
Italy **Itaria**

J

January **ichi-gatsu**
Japan **Nihon**; in Japan **Nihon de wa**
Japanese language **Nihongo**
job **shigoto**
juice **jūsu**
July **shichi-gatsu**
June **roku-gatsu**

K

kilometre **kiromētoru**
kiosk **kiosuku**

L

left (direction) **hidari**
lemon squash **remon jūsu**
lemon tea **remon tii**
letter **tegami**
library **toshokan**
lift **erebētā**
like: I like (tennis) **(tenisu) ga suki desu**
little: a little, small amount **sukoshi**
lobby **robii**
London **Rondon**
long: It's been a long time, hasn't it! **shibaraku desu ne**
lot: a lot of **takusan**
lounge **raunji**
lunch **ranchi, hirugohan**; lunch set menu **ranchi setto**

M

Malta **Maruta**
man **otoko (no hito)**
Manchester **Manchesutā**
many **takusan**
March **san-gatsu**
May **go-gatsu**
me **watashi**
meal **shokuji**

meat niku
melon meron
Mexico Mekishiko
milk miruku
minute -fun/-pun
mixed sandwich mikkusu sando
Monday getsuyōbi
more motto
Morning! ohayō
Mr, Mrs, Ms -san
my watashi no

N

name (o-)namae
nearby chikaku
Nepal Nepāru
new atarashii
newspaper shinbun
next tsugi no
next to tonari
nine kyū/ku
ninth (of the month) kokonoka
no iie
not: isn't; aren't ja arimasen (neg of desu), arimasen, imasen; am not ja arimasen (neg of desu), imasen
nought rei
November jū-ichi gatsu
now ima
number bangō

O

o'clock -ji
October jū-gatsu
of no
office worker kaishain
once ichido; once again mō ichido
one ichi; (when counting objects) hitotsu
one-way katamichi
open: to be open aite masu
opposite mukai, hantai
orange juice orenji jūsu

overnight: one overnight stay ip-paku
over there asoko

P

Paris Pari
park kōen
person, people hito; one person hitori; two people futari
phone denwa; phone extension number nai-sen bangō; phone number denwa bangō
pineapple painappuru
pizza piza
platform -ban sen; which platform? nan-ban sen
please onegai shimasu
pleased to meet you dōzo yoroshiku
police box kōban
pool pūru
pork cutlet tonkatsu
post office yūbinkyoku
postcard hagaki

R

rather (a little) chotto
Really? sō desu ka
really: not really, not very (with negative) amari
receipt ryōshūsho, reshiito
reception (hotel) furonto
reservation: made a reservation yoyaku shimashita
reserved seat shitei-seki
restaurant resutoran
return ticket ōfuku
rice (in a western-style restaurant) raisu; (in a Japanese restaurant) gohan
right (direction) migi; (correct): that's right sō desu

room heya; (Japanese-style) washitsu; (Western-style) yōshitsu

S

sandwich sando(icchi)
Saturday doyōbi
Scotland Sukottorando
seat: reserved seat shitei-seki; unreserved seat jiyū-seki
second (of the month) futsuka
September kū-gatsu
set meal setto
seven nana
seventh (of the month) nanoka
shiitake mushrooms shiitake
shoes kutsu
show: please show me misete kudasai
shower shawā
single room shinguru
six roku
sixth (of the month) muika
size saizu
slowly yukkuri; more slowly motto yukkuri
small chiisai
smell nioi
sports centre supōtsu senta
stamp kitte
steak sutēki
stereo sutereo
straight ahead massugu
student gakusei
Sunday nichiyōbi
Sweden Suēden

T

taxi takushii
tea (black) kōcha; tea with milk miruku tii
teacher (when addressing someone) sensei; (occupation) kyōshi

television **terebi**
ten **jū**
ten thousand **man**
tenth (of the month) **tōka**
Thailand **Tai**
thank you **arigatō**; thank you very much **arigatō gozaimasu**; thanks **dōmo**
that **sono**; that (one)/those (ones) **sore**; that (one)/those (ones) … over there **are**; that … over there **ano**
then (and also) **sore kara**
there **soko**
these **kono**; these (ones) **kore**
third (of the month) **mikka**
this **kono**; this (one) **kore**
thousand **sen**
three **san**; (when counting objects) **mittsu**
Thursday **mokuyōbi**
to(wards) **e**
toast **tōsuto**
toaster **tōsutā**
today **kyō**
tofu **tōfu**
toilet **toire**, (o-)tearai
tomato **tomato**
tomorrow **ashita**
too (also) **mo**

tourist information office **kankō annaijo**
towel **taoru**
traffic lights **shingō**
train **densha**; train station **eki**
Tuesday **kayōbi**
twentieth (of the month) **hatsuka**
twenty years old **hatachi**
twin room **tsuin**
two **ni**; (when counting objects) **futatsu**

U

understand: Do you understand? **wakarimasu ka**; I don't understand, I don't know **wakarimasen**

V

vending machine **jidō hanbaiki**

W

Wales **Uēruzu**
was **deshita**
watch **tokei**
weather **tenki**
Wednesday **suiyōbi**
welcome: you're welcome (in response to **arigatō**) **iie, dō itashimashite**

well (adv.) **ii**; (healthy) **genki**; Are you well? **(o-)genki desu ka**; well then **ja**
were **deshita**
what? **nani/nan**; what day? **nanyōbi**; what number? **nan-ban**; what time? **nan-ji**
when? **itsu**
where? **doko**; (polite) **dochira**
which? **dono**; which one/s **dore**
wife: (my) wife **kanai**, **tsuma**; (your) wife **okusan**
wine **wain**
woman **onna (no hito)**
workplace: your workplace **(o-)tsutome**

Y

years old **-sai**
yen **en**
yes **hai**, (informal) **ee**
young **wakai**

Z

zero **zero**